Confessions of an Instant Mom

A Foster-Adoption Story

Tina Miller, MSW

Confessions of an Instant Mom
published by Create Space

© 2017

Cover Design by: Tina Miller
Cover Photo by: Tina Miller

Published in the United States by Create Space.
ALL RIGHTS RESERVED

No part of this publication may be reproduced, stored in a retrieval system, or transmitted, in any form or by any means – electronic, mechanical, photocopying, recording, or otherwise – without written permission.

Miller, Tina Michelle
   Confessions of an Instant Mom/by Tina Miller, MSW.

ISBN-13: 978-1544839769
ISBN-10: 1544839766

1. Adoption. 2. Foster-Adoption. 3. Parenting. 4. Foster care.

Table of Contents

Introduction		9
Chapter 1	The year I got my period and my passion	12
Chapter 2	How do you start a family the non-old-fashioned way?	17
Chapter 3	Congratulations! You have bouncing pre-teen girls!	32
Chapter 4	The "infamous" Big and Little	39
Chapter 5	Ground rules	44
Chapter 6	Making up for lost time	60
Chapter 7	Ghost stories aren't just for Halloween	65
Chapter 8	More "infamous" Big and Little	86
Chapter 9	Don't drink the Kool-Aid	89
Chapter 10	A cabinet full of hair products	92
Chapter 11	Broken records	97
Chapter 12	Getting schooled	102
Chapter 13	Poking the momma bear	109
Chapter 14	FAQ's	116
Chapter 15	Finishing on a funny note	140

Acknowledgements

There are so many people I could list on the acknowledgements page. Let's be honest, they're probably the only ones who will read this page anyway. First, I have to thank my husband who suggested I write this book in the first place. Of course, there would be no book without my two amazing daughters, so I'm thankful for their permission to tell their story. I'm also thankful for their biological parents who made the difficult choice to sign the adoption papers willingly because they knew that a permanent, loving home was something they couldn't offer to their children. Our family wouldn't have come together without the caseworkers and others who were involved with our case and helped make our adoption happen. Specifically, I need to mention our amazing, fun, and brilliant adoption caseworker, Sarah Withrow, who offered her wisdom to the writing of this book. Finally, I need to acknowledge all the amazing parents who have set such a wonderful example for what healthy parenting looks like, including my own parents.

Introduction

Over the years, my choice to adopt has been met with a variety of reactions and questions. Some people react with amazement, some pity, and a few have even reacted with skepticism. My decision to adopt is hardly as altruistic or amazing as people may assume and our situation is definitely not as pitiful as some people suspect.

As for skepticism, I think some people watch too many horror movies featuring adopted children. Rest assured, my children haven't put strychnine in the well, stolen our money, or attempted to murder us in our sleep. In fact, my adopted children are a lot nicer than some of the biological children I see with their parents in the grocery store.

Adoption is a lot less mysterious than most people assume, but it is challenging and definitely not something I would recommend for just anyone who wants to expand their family.

There are several different ways to put a family together through adoption, including domestic adoption of infants, international adoption of infants, private adoptions, guardianship, international adoption of older children, and adoption through the foster care system.

My husband and I chose to adopt older children through the foster care system. We were older when we got married and didn't think we had the energy to parent a baby at our "advanced" age (late-30's). Plus, older kids sometimes get stuck in the foster care system because there aren't enough adoptive families willing to take kids who already have opinions and habits gained from a difficult life. Many adoptive families see older kids as "too risky" and think infants are more of a blank slate. Having worked in the school system for many years, I knew that kids want to be kids and sometimes they just need the right home life to give them that opportunity.

I think now is the right time to tell you that I'm sometimes a control freak. I like to know what is coming and study it until I understand it before taking the first step. When my husband and I were stepping into the adoption process, I began looking for as much information as I could find about parenting older kids from the foster care system. While I did find a couple of blogs with a few posts on the topic, it was hard to find the depth of information or advice to would help us adequately prepare for such a giant leap into parenting.

Hopefully this book will provide some answers, advice, and maybe some laughs as I share what my family has learned together through adopting older children in foster care. My experience is certainly not everyone's experience and my parenting style is hardly perfect. But, maybe our insight will give you just a little hope that foster-adoption might be possible for your family.

Chapter 1
The year I got my period and my passion

The year was 1985 and I was a twelve-year old living in a small, rural town in Missouri. Our whole class had been shuffled by gender into separate classrooms two years earlier to get the "hygiene talk", so I knew what was coming. I knew that "Aunt Flow" wasn't going to stay away forever; that eventually I would get boobs and my period like most of the other girls in my class. And I was right. January of that year was when I got my first period and my eyes were officially opened to the atrocities of womanhood.

In church I had learned all about Adam and Eve and how it was mostly Eve's fault that they ate the fruit from that one bad tree. I learned that Eve was the reason we have "pain in childbirth", so I assumed she was also to blame for cramps, greasy skin, and embarrassing period "accidents".

That year-I-was-twelve was also the year I started to understand about childbirth. There were some young women at my church who were pregnant or having their first child and they were not shy about sharing the awful (and, might I add, emotionally-scarring) details of pregnancy and childbirth. Hearing them talk about it was like watching a slasher movie, and I imagined that babies had knives for fingernails to claw their way out of a woman's vagina. They told stories about pooping during childbirth, of something called the "Ring of Fire", and the giant, sore nipples from breastfeeding. It all sounded terrible and terrifying and was definitely not something I was interested in trying. *Ever.*

The-year-I-was-twelve was also the year I saw a "20/20" special about Eastern European orphanages where children languished day in and day out trapped in cribs without ever being held; living out a loveless childhood as they failed to thrive. Many of these too-small orphans looked disgustingly malnourished, like forgotten animals in cages.

I remember watching that episode of "20/20" and sobbing through the entire thing. The only other time I cried that hard was when I listened to Foreigner's "I Wanna Know What Love Is" and cried about that boy in my class who didn't *like*-like me.

My devastation over those foreign orphans on TV was a life-changing moment in my young life. My eyes were opened for the first time to a desperate need in the world. I knew at age twelve that there were too many children in the world and not enough parents to raise them. It was that year when I made my decision to adopt my children, rather than giving birth.

Sometime later in my teenage years I learned about child abuse and neglect, and about children who bounce around the foster care system for years. While my friends were thinking about what boyfriend-on-girlfriend action they could get away with when our teachers weren't watching, I was concerned about how to stem the tide of lifelong issues caused by thousands of children who have no place to call "home". I was no saint as a teenager, but I was definitely not happy to simply move from high school into the labor and delivery suite like so many of my classmates seemed to be.

Because I grew up in a small town, most of the people around me had dreams of graduating from high school, getting married and starting their family right away. It's what girls did in our area of the country. Women held an important role in our farming community as they raised the boys who would take over their fathers' farms someday.

But, I didn't grow up on a farm. My dad was an engineer and my mother a writer. I didn't have a farm to pass down, nor did I have a desire to marry into such a dream. I didn't fit in with the dreams of the girls sitting around me in my classes.

"Oh, you'll change your mind someday" and other phrases that never get old

As I grew closer to high school graduation, people would often ask questions related to those kinds of marriage-and-family dreams. "Who are you dating?", "Do you have a boyfriend yet?" and "Are there any serious fellas in your life?" were questions asked more often than "Which colleges have you applied to?"

I vividly remember several conversations during my teenage years where my reproductive plans were part of the discussion. I'm not sure why adults outside my immediate family needed to know when I was planning to have a baby even though I wasn't even old enough to vote. I do remember my answer – and their predictable reaction. Most of the time when I told people my plans to adopt, I was met with "Oh, you'll change your mind after you fall in love. Trust me, someday you'll want to have a baby who looks like your husband."

Luckily, I'm pretty independent and stubborn. It didn't matter that people thought I would change my mind because I had the strength of my conviction to drive my choices rather than the opinions of others.

I could have changed my mind and that would have been okay. Having children the "old-fashioned way" is certainly not a bad thing and, despite my secret babies-with-knife-claws fear, I'm sure I could have given birth to my children if I had the inclination. This book is definitely not about shaming someone for choosing biology over adoption.

In fact, I will be the first one to tell the world that adoption isn't for everyone. I have known several couples who have struggled for years with infertility. They went through all the treatments, hormone injections, ovulation calendars, old wives' tales, and expensive alternatives. I've seen their pain, desperation, sadness, and the crazy-eyes that came with their high-priced hormone shots.

Fertility isn't an easy struggle and it is devastating to have tried all the options without success. But, that doesn't mean that anyone should push adoption as the only solution. It isn't helpful to meet someone's grief over losing the fertility battle with a slew of adoption pamphlets or a Pollyanna-ish message about how their babies are probably just waiting in orphanages or foster care. Adoption isn't meant to fill the hole in someone's life that has come from being unable to conceive or carry a biological child.

And adoption isn't some altruistic endeavor that people should take on just because they feel sorry for orphans or kids in foster care. If you feel sorry for a child in foster care, certainly pray about how you might be able to help, but don't open your home unless you are 100% ready to deal with all that comes along with bringing a hurting child into your life. You cannot compare adoption to having children through biology because the challenges are unique and I would hate for you to expect it to be easy.

Most people arrive at their decision to adopt at a different pace and in a different way than I did. My year-I-was-twelve experience is definitely not the usual way people arrive at the decision to adopt.

Here is my list of the most important things to consider before entering the foster-to-adopt world:

- Is my spouse (and the rest of my immediate family) 100% on board with this decision?
- Do I have a support network to encourage me and help out?
- Am I patient enough to deal with a child who has challenging behavior?
- Do I have a good handle on my own negative reactions when my buttons are pushed?
- Do I have the parenting skills it will take to provide a stable, consistent home life with a routine and rules on which the child can rely?
- Do I have the time to commit to this kind of parenting situation, such as if the child still has weekly mandatory visits with their biological family or visits with a therapist?
- Am I willing to let other people into my life, like caseworkers, therapists, CASA volunteers, and lawyers?
- Can I endure the process of becoming and remaining foster-licensed as I go through this process?

- ❏ Do I have the patience and time to track down all the records I will need in order to understand my child's history and current needs?
- ❏ Am I willing to patiently answer people's questions or deflect their inappropriate comments regarding my child(ren) or our family?
- ❏ Am I willing to deal with my adopted child's grief and loss, which will come in waves as they move through different stages of maturity?
- ❏ Can I answer my child's questions about their biological family without throwing their biological parents completely under the bus?
- ❏ Am I really, truly prepared to love a child who isn't biologically related to me?

If you can't make it through this list, you should probably put down this book, walk away from the decision to adopt through the foster care system, and pick up something more entertaining to read.

Chapter 2
How do you start a family the non-old-fashioned way?

A lot of people ask me about our adoption process. Only a small number of these people are asking because they are interested in choosing to adopt their own children someday. Most people who ask are curious because the concept of adoption is foreign to them. Perhaps they have had only biological children and can't imagine loving a child who wasn't born to them. Or maybe they have heard adoption nightmares (or have watched horror movies) and wonder if our adoption fits their suspicions that all adoptions are tumultuous.

The decision
First off, we adopted older children through the foster care system, which will be the focus of this book. I know there are many avenues for adoption; this is the one we chose. For us adoption was an intentional choice to start our family (not a secondary option due to infertility). As I said in chapter one, I have always had a heart for children who are stuck in lousy situations, waiting for a family. Since the year I was twelve I have always been keenly aware of children languishing in orphanages or trapped in the cycle of a broken foster care system.

At any given time there are approximately 415,000 kids in foster care in the United States. Of those, half are reunited with their parents and a quarter will be adopted (often by their foster parents). Approximately 20,000 kids "age out" of the system each year because their parents were never able to meet reunification goals and no adoptive home was available. One-third of kids in foster care will average three different placements and another third will average eight different placements. The average stay in foster care is just over 28 months. (Statistics: *U.S. Children's Bureau*, 2016)

The statistics are not pretty for the outcome of kids who

have suffered child abuse and neglect. About one-third will grow up to abuse their own children and the rates for substance abuse, violent crime, and arrest rates would make you cry. Kids who endure that kind of childhood don't have much hope of a happy adulthood without some significant intervention. (Statistics: *Centers for Disease Control and Prevention*, 2016)

When I entered into a serious relationship with my now-husband, adoption first became a conversation and then a promise. He had a rough childhood with alcoholic parents and multiple moves to avoid trouble with various landlords. Luckily, he had some good people along the way who helped him overcome the negative habits and anger from his early life. My husband's early experiences left him with a desire to make a difference in the lives of kids who have experienced the same kinds of difficulties he did as a kid. Adopting kids from the foster care system became a natural fit once we began having those serious soon-to-be-married conversations.

My husband and I both agreed that older children in foster care are the most vulnerable population. There are countless couples and individuals ready to take adorable little infants and toddlers who are available for adoption. Long waiting lists for private and foster adoptions prove this fact. Many couples wait up to two years before being matched with an infant – some even longer than that.

My own anecdotal evidence from conversations over the years suggests that many people see infants and toddlers as less risky in adoption because they had less exposure to unhealthy parenting. While this can be true, adopting infants and toddlers is risky in other ways because potential mental illness won't show itself in such young children and many infants who enter foster care have been exposed to prenatal substance abuse. Even so, many people feel that infants and toddlers are more of a blank slate, more able to accept healthy parenting in the adoptive home than older children. Because of this perceived risk, older children tend to spend much longer waiting for adoptive parents.

First step: the foster-licensing process

After several years of marriage, my husband and I decided it was time to add the chaos of children to our family.

We began the process by contacting our local Children's Division office. Children's Division is what they call it in Missouri. Other states use names like "Division of Children and Families" or "Department of Human Services". I'll use the Missouri terminology and process in this book because I doubt you want to read a super-boring book detailing the process in fifty different states. Plus, I think such a tedious tome would require me to change the name to "The Never-Ending Story" and you probably wouldn't keep reading past this sentence.

Each state has a slightly different process, but not dramatically different from what Missouri uses. For specific details about your state, the Internet provides a wealth of initial information and I highly recommend contacting your local child protection agency to speak with an adoption caseworker. They are often more than happy to answer questions and usually won't pressure anyone to begin the process if they aren't comfortable.

The caseworker we contacted at Children's Division sent us the initial application. We submitted it and were then placed us on the roster for an upcoming foster parent training session. In the state of Missouri, adults who wish to adopt through the foster care system must first pass through the process to become foster-licensed. This process in Missouri is called *Specialized Training Assessment Resources and Support (S.T.A.R.S.)* and involves 27 hours of classes. It may be taught in different increments depending on how accelerated they want to make it or based on instructor availability. Our particular session stretched over nine weeks. S.T.A.R.S. is the same thing as *Parent Resources for Information, Development and Education (P.R.I.D.E.)* in several other states, but we stubborn Missourians changed the name.

During the weeks of training, adults will also complete a background check and a couple of stages of home study. During our initial home study, a social worker from Children's Division walked through our home looking at all the areas that were red flags (like needing plug covers, buying a fire-extinguisher, locking our medicine cabinet, and having a safety plan for our kitchen knives). Some things were expected, like making sure our smoke detectors worked. Other things weren't on our radar, like locking up our lawnmower gasoline. It was like playing a terrifying game of "1,000 Ways to Be Murdered in your Sleep" as we looked at all the items in our house and had to think about how they could be deadly in the hands of a highly disturbed child. We had a few weeks to fix the issues and she returned to complete the initial round of the home study process.

The second round of home study was very thorough and extremely intense. A social worker spent about six hours with us, taking a thorough history of our own childhoods, educational and work history, how we were disciplined, and any troublesome behaviors (sexual abuse in the past, drug use, addiction, etc.). It felt a little like psychotherapy, only it didn't solve our problems or making us feel better.

The S.T.A.R.S. classes themselves were easy but not especially interesting (that's a nice way to put it). The point of the classes seemed to be weeding out the people who had wrong motives or unrealistic expectations about fostering. Most of the topics in the training focused on all the challenges of foster parenting – mental illness, challenging behaviors, educational issues, learning disabilities, health problems, stealing food, dealing with the biological parents, and managing all the foster requirements. If someone is planning to be a foster parent just for the monthly stipends, the S.T.A.R.S. classes are meant to help them see that it's a lousy way to make money.

By the time we (finally) reached the last class session, we lost at least one-third of the participants in our S.T.A.R.S. cohort. Confession time: I spent some of the time in our S.T.A.R.S. classes wondering how some of the couples stumbled into the foster-licensing process in the first place. It was like the parenting version of *American Idol* auditions where some tone-deaf loon seems to genuinely believe they will be selected for the show. My husband and I suspected that several participants dropped out because they didn't pass the background check and several others were scared off by the intense way our instructors described some children's behavior.

Second step: the adoption-licensing process

After we completed the S.T.A.R.S. sessions, we were funneled into the next step of the process. For adults interested in adopting a foster child in Missouri, an additional set of courses is required. The courses we were required to take were called Spaulding and took two weeks (another 12 hours of classes). Other states call it *Adopt P.R.I.D.E.*, but Missouri wasn't happy to leave the name alone and calls it *S.T.A.R.S. Making the Commitment to Adopt: Spaulding*, although no one calls it by that long name.

Again, the point of this process seemed to be weeding out those folks who were only vaguely committed, had grossly unrealistic expectations, or who had wrong motives.

In fact, I think learning about our expectations and motives was the main goal of the very first activity we did in our first Spaulding session. The instructor's question for us seemed innocent enough, "Write down a description of the adopted child you dream about."

Most people had lovely dreams of their future adopted foster baby or their hope of adopting a sweet teenager. One guy in our class jokingly suggested that his dream adopted-child was "a 40-year old man who loves to do yard work". It got a hearty laugh out of the class and even the instructor appreciated the joke.

Seriously, though...there are people who foster/adopt children for the express purpose of "hiring" free labor. And by "free labor" I mean slaves. I'm not talking about the kid who does their fair share of work on the family farm along with everyone else in the household. Those kinds of work-alongside-the-family experiences can build character, work ethic, job skills, and self-esteem.

If you're reading this book, dreaming of a child who can work in your basement sweatshop or shave your bunions for you, then you might want to find something else to read.

And if you're planning to foster or adopt so you can make porn videos of your "children" then put down this book and turn yourself in to the police, you sick-o.

The hard, sad truth about foster-adoption

If I had to sum up the licensing process into one sentence it would be: Adopting a child through the foster care system is not for the weak.

The children "in the system" are there for a reason – namely because they have parents who were either grossly unable to provide adequate care or had some abhorrent, illegal behavior (like sexual abuse, physical abuse, or drug exposure). While some families enter the system due to temporary, easy-to-remedy challenges, that's not usually the case.

Many of the biological parents with kids in the system are what you might consider "a hot mess" and the homes they keep are nightmarishly filthy. I won't try to shock you with detailed descriptions of these homes because you would probably just close this book and go scrub your whole body with bleach.

The children who enter state custody most often have challenging behavior due to the things they have experienced, such as:

- ✓ 80% of kids in foster care experienced neglect
- ✓ Lack of consistent, healthy food – and maybe even periods of intense hunger
- ✓ Lack of medical care for basic needs resulting in skin infections, failure to thrive, or other problems
- ✓ Lack of a bed to sleep in or too many people sleeping together in the same bed, resulting in the child getting inadequate sleep each night
- ✓ Lack of clean clothes because soap and the laundromat

cost money that parents need for other bills and/or alcohol, cigarettes and drugs
- ✓ Entire family units may sleep in the same room, which means children may have seen adults having sex in front of them
- ✓ Lack of basic necessities for hygiene like soap, toothpaste and deodorant
- ✓ Exposure to drugs and/or drug production chemicals
- ✓ Pest infestations like cockroaches, fleas, and mice
- ✓ Children might have a history of untreated head lice and scabies
- ✓ Biological mom or dad (or their paramours) have physically abused the child and/or siblings in 18% of cases
- ✓ 9% of kids in foster care have been sexually abused (although that number is likely *much* higher)
- ✓ Emotional abuse is the norm for many kids before they enter foster care
- ✓ Neglect means that a child may have been responsible to care for themselves and younger siblings with no adult assistance
- ✓ Pornographic materials may be easily accessible to children in the home or, in some cases, there has been intentional exposure to sexual materials
- ✓ Medications, alcohol, cigarettes, illegal drugs, and toxic chemicals may be easily accessible by even small children in the home
- ✓ Living conditions may not include working heat, air-conditioning, or utilities
- ✓ Parents may not pay for trash service, instead allowing trash to pile up in and around every portion of the home
- ✓ The child may have witnessed crimes their parent(s) committed
- ✓ Biological parents often routinely lie to children
- ✓ Biological parents often parent out of guilt, buying their child candy, sodas, or other junk to make up for all their

other parenting failures
- ✓ Parents may not have any behavioral expectations or discipline strategies for misbehavior and may never tell a child "no"
- ✓ Many children have mental health concerns as a result of abuse, drug exposure, or genetics (or a combination of the three)
- ✓ Other concerns might contribute to behaviors, which may be discussed with your individual caseworker
(Statistics: *National Children's Alliance*, 2014)

Due to these and other unhealthy lifestyle habits of the biological home, children often enter foster care with many unhealthy habits born out of hunger, filth, and lack of boundaries. They often have many unpleasant behaviors in the beginning. They may hoard food because are insecure about when they might see their next meal. Or they may throw violent tantrums when things don't go the way they planned. Some children steal, lie, respond with violence, or use curse words. Other, more troubled children, might harm family pets, rub their feces on the walls, or urinate in inappropriate places around the home.

Our experience with children from the foster care system was very ideal and that has also been the case for most of our friends who have fostered or adopted through the state. In all of our time in the system, we experienced none of the really terrible things that were reported in the classes we took.

But, we know that those things do exist due to the very troubling things that some adults do to harm children. In fact, one couple from our adoption class ended up fostering a group of siblings, including a child who had been raped repeatedly starting at age six months. She had also been shaken repeatedly by an angry parent trying to stop her from crying. The injuries she received from her abuse caused mental and physical disabilities that will likely be life-long. Thankfully, the couple who fostered that sibling group had a medical background and previous experience with physical disabilities. They were more than prepared for the challenges they faced with that particular placement.

Adopting from the foster system means being prepared to accept the unhealthy behaviors and other challenges children bring with them and helping them learn new ways to cope. More on that in a few chapters.

Being matched for adoption is like finding love on Tinder only completely different

Once we went through the foster parent and adoption licensing process, we were available to be matched with children who were available for adoption.

After completing the whole process, my husband and I chose to be considered "adopt only" foster parents. What that means is that our home was considered closed to foster children except for those children we were matched with for adoption. We didn't receive calls in the middle of the night to accept foster placements, although we did accept a few short-term respite placements while we waited for our adoption caseworker to match us with a child. All the placements we took were 100% on our terms and within our comfort level.

Our experience is not what all foster families experience, however. I know there were people in our initial round of foster parent classes who brought children home on the day of our final class because workers were so desperate for new homes to become available. There are other people in our circle of influence whose homes were maxed out (meaning they had the maximum allowable number of children in their home) and they still received calls from caseworkers asking them to temporarily accept just one more. Bottom Line: the system is broken and there aren't enough available families to take all the children who need care.

The goal of foster care is to reunite children with their biological parents whenever possible. While children stay with a foster parent, caseworkers and others work with the biological parents to change problem behaviors. For example, if a child was removed from the home due to drug use by the parents, then the child will not be returned home until the parent has met certain goals to be drug-free.

This process can take months or even years. While President, Bill Clinton passed legislation that limited the amount of time children could remain in foster care. If parents aren't successful at meeting goals (or at least making reasonable progress toward their goals) within a fifteen month time period, the goal can be changed to find a permanent home for the child. To say a child is "available" for adoption means that the case goal has been changed from reunification to adoption. Eventually, if biological parents do not make necessary changes, the parental rights can be legally terminated by a judge.

In Missouri, children whose case goal has been changed to adoption are generally considered "legal risk" adoptive placements. Often, a judge will not terminate the parental rights until an appropriate adoptive placement has been chosen.

Until rights have been terminated, the biological parents still have some legal rights to their children. They can hire a lawyer and fight the adoption process. For this reason, the process often moves very slowly and is very drawn out. The government does not want to be seen as stealing children from biological families and giving them away without a great deal of evidence that it truly was in the child's best interest.

Caseworkers walk a tightrope in this process and prospective parents must be aware of the sticky situation into which they are stepping. In any event, the case team and judge want to make a solid case that termination of parental rights and adoption is the best option to provide a permanent home for a child.

The process of matching parents to available children was an interesting one for us. While going through the adoption licensing process, our caseworker suggested we make an adoption life book. This book would be used to "sell" ourselves to caseworkers working with available children. In our case, I created a book using the website Shutterfly and I got several copies printed with soft covers (like a paperback book). Our life book contained pictures of us, our dog, our home, and information about our career, hobbies, and other fun facts.

Caseworkers from across the state communicate with each other when children become available for adoption (when their case goal has been changed from reunification to adoption).

Our caseworker knew what kind of children we were looking for. My husband and I were interested in adopting a sibling group of up to four children who were age 5 - 14. Because she had gotten to know us personally throughout the adoption licensing process, our caseworker had a good idea of our personality and interests. As she received adoption profiles for available children, she kept in mind which kids might be a good fit for our home and she sent us their profiles to see if we wanted to take the next step in the match process. For those we chose to be matched with, our caseworker would send the child's caseworker a copy of our adoption profile along with our adoption life book.

Over the course of six months, we were matched with three different sibling groups. The first match we were offered was with a set of siblings a county about an hour away from where we live. We received a brief profile on each child in the sibling group. This profile gave their age, gender, and a brief summary of their personality. The profile also listed a summary of known health, mental health and educational issues.

We agreed to be interviewed as a potential placement and were given an interview date and time. This meeting included our adoption caseworker and the caseworker for the children, along with the guardian ad litem (the children's lawyer) and a couple of other professionals who had been working with the children's case. It felt a little like a job interview.

After interviewing all the prospective parents, the caseworker ended up choosing someone else. We found out later that one of the children was a key witness to their parents' highly-publicized crime and the situation surrounding this sibling group would involve ongoing legal contact with the case.

We were matched with a second set of siblings in a county about three hours from where we live. The interview was much different for this set of siblings. From what we could tell, the caseworker wasn't interviewing anyone other than my husband and me. I'm not sure whether that's due to our awesomeness (on paper, anyway) or that she didn't want to bother with too many interviews. Unfortunately, aside from not wanting to consider all the options, that caseworker was also very disorganized. It was like the casework version of a junior high boy.

Things started to disintegrate almost immediately after we entered the interview room. The caseworker's lack of organization had opened the door for a biological relative (who had previously been ruled out as a prospective parent due to her advanced age) to fight for one of the three siblings. Other issues quickly surfaced during the meeting. It was like pulling a lose thread and unraveling the whole, ugly sweater in the process.

We left the interview with a mixture of relief and exhaustion and told our adoption caseworker to remove our name from consideration for this particular sibling group. Even though the case team wanted to select us, we were not interested in stepping into such a messy, disorganized case. It didn't feel like a good fit and our caseworker wasn't interested in forcing something that might not be a successful placement.

Our third potential placement was "introduced" to us on the day before Halloween of 2012. We received an adoption profile for two sweet-sounding sisters from a county about four hours from where we live. After several emails back and forth between our caseworker, the girls' caseworker and eventually the girls' foster parent, we were set to attend our third adoption interview several weeks later.

We interviewed on December 17, and everyone in the room seemed to have the same sense that this was the right choice. The next day we received the good news that we were selected as the adoptive parents. Two days after that we drove back to meet the girls for the first time. Nine days after that we brought them home for good.

In Missouri, the child must reside in the pre-adoptive home for six months prior to adoption. The state still retains legal custody of the child during that time period. In our case it took longer than six months because there were some issues in the process to legally terminate the parental rights.

Eventually, both biological parents voluntarily signed the termination paperwork and we were given an adoption date in November of 2013.

Adoption Day

Just like a pregnancy filled with morning sickness and eventually followed by a 36-hour labor, nothing was as smooth as we hoped in our adoption process. There was a lot of waiting, wondering and praying. During one meeting with the caseworker we might receive one answer, which would later be contradicted by the Court-Appointed Special Advocate (CASA). Court date after court date would happen with seemingly no action in the case. It went from the six months we hoped for and dragged on; testing my patience at every turn. It's a bit like being 40 weeks pregnant and finding out the doctor can't schedule your delivery for three more months.

We began the adoption classes in January 2012, met our children almost a full calendar year later, and didn't become legal parents until November of 2013. As someone who lacks patience, this process was a lot longer than I really expected and it sometimes felt like someone had pushed the pause button on our lives.

It was a huge relief when we finally reached our adoption court date. In Missouri, adoption court happens in the county where the child entered into state custody, because that court has had jurisdiction over the child for the entirety of the case. In our situation, that was four hours away from where we live.

When we finally received our adoption court date, our caseworker gave us the name of the one lawyer in that county who worked with the family laws related to adoption. Many larger counties have more options for lawyers, but this small county had only one guy they generally worked with. I was given his contact information and got in touch with him to file the paperwork officially. It turned out our lawyer was a lovely man who had kids and grandkids. His office was decorated with Walt Disney World paraphernalia from his many trips, which made him much more approachable. He asked a lot of questions to make sure everything was filed correctly.

Many of the questions our lawyer asked related to filing the forms to receive new birth certificates. One thing I didn't realize about adoptions is that children are issued a new birth certificate after adoption is finalized. This is partly due to Missouri being a closed-adoption state, but partly to reflect their new identity. As it turns out, the girls now have birth certificates with my husband and me listed as their birth parents, which is ironic because my husband and I hadn't even met each other when either girl was born. It makes for a strange reality in adoption, but also gives us a great answer to use whenever we play "Two Truths and a Lie".

The county where our adoption happened has a limited number of adoption court sessions on the calendar each month. They do this so that children and families won't have to mingle with criminals in the court waiting areas. Our particular judge hosts adoption court right after the lunch recess to ensure that no one is in the courthouse other than regular court staff and those individuals present for adoption proceedings. It made for a very safe, inviting experience. Each judge is a little different in their procedures for adoption court.

In addition to our family, all the adoption case team came to our court appointment. They brought gifts and their cameras because they were excited to document the happy side of this case. One caseworker told me that there are lots of hard moments in their job, but adoptions are some of the good moments that make it all worthwhile.

After opening presents and greeting the girls' case team members, the judge began the proceedings. He didn't use the gavel, which I was actually looking forward to since that's how it always happens on TV. He called my husband and me up to the stand to state, under oath, that we would provide for the girls' needs and treat them as our own children, just as if they had been born to us. Then the judge addressed the girls to ask if they were happy about being adopted (they were, I'm glad to report). He read the adoption decree and pronounced the adoption final. We ended with about a hundred photos of us and the judge.

I won't say adoption court is a barrel of laughs, but it was definitely a special experience I will never forget. Plus, I've got to say that adopting my children was a heckuva lot better than pushing a baby with knife-claws out of my vagina.

Chapter 3
Congratulations! You have bouncing pre-teen girls!

We got daughters for Christmas of 2012.

The funny thing about the foster-adopt process is you make a life-long decision based on a paragraph. Or two if you're lucky. The caseworkers write these vague profiles and often don't include pictures. You are asked to decide if you want to submit your home study to be considered as their adoptive parents, sight-unseen. I would never in a million years buy a car or even a pair of shoes this way, but that's how the adoption process works when you go through the foster care system. We agreed to be their parents before we ever even met them. Talk about a strange feeling.

Due to the timing of things, we met the girls for the first time at the beginning of Christmas Break and the plan was to go back a week later to bring them home permanently, after they had celebrated Christmas with their foster family. That was a pretty fast transition and the case team was nervous about moving so quickly. We went ahead with the quick timeline so the girls could change schools at the start of the new semester. We decided that minimizing school disruptions was a good reason to accelerate the timeline.

When we took our adoption classes, our instructors told us about all the tricky situations in the fostering and adoption process. There were warnings about Reactive Attachment Disorder and behavior problems and head lice and bizarre behaviors that some foster kids exhibit. But, no one told us about all the sweet moments we might experience in the transition from foster to adoption.

The first sweet moment was the night we met the girls. They had received our life book earlier that week and had, apparently, spent the week studying and memorizing every page. When we met the girls they excitedly recounted all the details they already knew about us. "Your favorite color is green!" "You love ice cream!" "Your favorite princess is Belle from *Beauty and the Beast!*" They were so excited to finally meet us and their enthusiasm was endearing. We left that first meeting already in love with these two sweet girls.

Our official "Gotcha Day" was on December 29th. Note: Some people use "Gotcha Day" to describe their adoption day, since that's the day their family was "official". We like dessert, so we are always looking for extra reasons to celebrate. In our family we do Gotcha Day for the anniversary of the day they came into our home and a separate Adoption Day for the anniversary of the day we went to court to make our adoption final.

December 29th was the day we drove back to meet them, along with their foster parents, so we could finally bring them home. They came with a LOT of stuff. I've never seen so many clothes. And Barbies. And purses.

We had rooms already prepared for children, so it was easy to move the girls in once the decision was made. Their girly stuff fit right in to the stuff we had already purchased, like bedding and pillows.

Lots of sweet moments followed as they came home, but the transition to forever began to feel real a few weeks into our lives together. That was the day they sweetly asked if they could call us "Mom" and "Dad". We had been out running errands and they were whispering with each other while we were checking out at the grocery store. My husband and I assumed they were plotting to get us to take them out for ice cream or to buy them candy. Sugar always seems to be their go-to whim purchase.

When we got home, Little Sister and I were in the kitchen making dinner. She asked, "Is it okay if we call you 'Mom' and 'Dad'?" When I answered "yes", she excitedly said "Yay! [Big Sister] and I were talking about it and we want to!"

It took a day or two after that for them to transition to our new titles and we have been Mom and Dad ever since. Not long after that, they started calling my parents "Grandma" and "Grandpa". It was a very organic, genuine change that happened. Nothing had to be forced, which made it all the more sweet.

About a month after they came home, they started having a conversation about changing their last names. Little Sister wondered about changing her middle name too and the conversation evolved from there into a discussion about changing their whole names. A couple of days later they asked if we could look on the Internet at possible names. With a little guidance, they picked out lovely new names and never wavered in their choice to make the change. And by guidance I mean that neither girl picked a name like "Candy Sparkle", "Cocoa Fluffykitty", or "Miley Cyrus".

Our transition process was very smooth, although I'm not sure how typical it was. The girls' final foster parents had taken them to see a therapist to help begin the adoption transition process before new parents were ever selected. The girls were helped in the transition process by receiving our life books to study before they ever met us in person. We continued the process by finding a therapist in our city to continue the work of helping them through the transition to a new home, new school, and new identity as our children. It wasn't all rainbows, sparkles and unicorns as you'll see if you keep reading; but it was much more smooth than I worried it might be.

"Instant Parenthood" would be a hilarious reality TV show

Our own transition from childless adults to full-fledged parents was a little less smooth. I used to love instant soup. Just add water and stir for a minute, then - Voila! - warm, salty goodness in a cup. That word "instant" applies to the early period of our transition into parenthood. In December of 2012 I became an "instant mom". My husband and I brought home our two daughters after Christmas and immediately became the parents of two Justin-Bieber loving, sparkly pink wearing, elementary students. On a related note: I'm happy to update you that the girls are no longer Beliebers.

Pre-kids we were that couple who could watch whatever we wanted, eat whenever we felt like, go out for ice cream on a whim and who could manage regular "romantic" time [wink-wink]. Now, we are that family who rarely changes the channel from "tween" shows, we hide our ice cream behind the frozen broccoli, and we sometimes plan our lives like bedtime is the only thing that really matters in life.

I love my girls, but it was a real change for us as a couple. Maybe other parents don't feel this way, but here are some confessions I wrote down in a journal from that time period:

- ✓ I'm pretty tired. Even if I get in bed at the right time, I have to get up early enough to get me *and* the girls ready. My husband is great, but he really isn't that great at picking out clothes that match or fixing hair so that it doesn't look like wild animals are nesting inside of it. That means that by 9:30 p.m. my eyes are drooping.
- ✓ I can see why couples generally start family planning at a younger age, because children take a lot of energy. And sometimes I don't feel that energetic. Sometimes I even put in a movie I know they'll want to watch just because I need a minute to breath. Or to poop alone.
- ✓ I really like going to the bathroom in peace. And that doesn't happen a lot anymore. I'm surprised by that with elementary-age children. I really thought I'd have more bathroom privacy than this. Invariably as soon as I release my bladder I hear "Mom?!" When I don't answer right away I hear "Mom? Mom?! MOM!" until I finally have to yell "I'M IN THE BATHROOM!" Sheesh, can't a mom just have 30 seconds without a question or request? On a related note: Why do my children continue to ask for *me* when my husband is sitting right there in the room with them?
- ✓ Having children has *really* changed my relationship with my husband. I refer to him as "dad" more often than I use his real name. Why do I do that? He's not *my* dad. But, I guess that's

how it goes when you have children. Plus we have very little time each day when we can to speak to each other like adults. There are always ears listening. The same children who claim they never heard us tell them to turn the TV off can hear my husband whisper to me that we should eat ice cream after the girls are asleep. From three rooms away. So we've chosen to keep most of our adult conversations in the confines of our bedroom after the girls are both safely tucked to sleep. Which means we have approximately 37 seconds of quality conversation before one or both of us start fighting against droopy eyelids.

- ✓ Now that we have children, my husband and I rarely sit next to each other at meals, on the couch, at the movie theatre or anywhere else. We used to hold hands with one another, but that now only happens in the car, primarily because neither girl is old enough to ride in the front seat (thank you Jesus for giving us airbags). Because of our particular adoption situation, the girls are mildly traumatized whenever we leave them with grandparents or a babysitter, so we don't choose to do that very often. Basically I really miss my husband, but this too shall pass.
- ✓ Girls are a lot more dramatic than I remember being when I was a girl. We have been surprised on numerous occasions so far with just how dramatic girls can be. One might melt into tears because the wrong person was picked to get her hair done first. Or another might melt into tears because we chose the other sister to hit the button to close the garage door. The most recent meltdown happened because one sister was allowed to carry a box of nails to the counter at the hardware store. Who knew that the hardware store could be a source of my-life-is-over tears?
- ✓ Girl drama can strike at any time. It's a little like a grumpy cobra. I guess I thought I understood girls, since I am one. But, sisters have a completely different relationship with each other than brothers and sisters do. I had a brother growing up and we definitely fought, but usually a brawl worked it out

and then we could move on. Sisters fight with much more manipulation and emotional warfare than they do physical fights. Something that we thought was resolved two weeks ago often rears its head again and again as new scuffles erupt.

I'm starting with the mom in the mirror

These aren't the only things that surprised me as an instant mom. I actually was most surprised by myself. I had a reaction to the adoption process that I didn't expect I would have. I have always wanted to adopt my children and have openly been sharing that plan since I was twelve years old. However, for the first few months of having the girls in our home, I found myself surprisingly embarrassed.

Let's be clear – I wasn't embarrassed of the girls. They were wonderful, even when they were fighting with each other and they still are. But I found myself feeling like I needed to explain our family to others. Of my two girls, one looks like she could have been born from my genetics. We have very similar hair and skin. People usually assume she is my biological child. The other daughter is biracial and her luscious caramel skin definitely does not resemble my pale whiteness. People notice my oldest daughter right away and sometimes they stare at us awkwardly. I don't mind the staring so much now, but I wasn't adequately prepared for it in those early months.

Add to that the awkwardness I felt when people asked the girls' names. Before the adoption happened, their last names were different from each other...and from me. Whenever I introduced them using their previous last names, I felt like I got a very particular reaction from others. A judgmental reaction. I could almost hear the other person thinking: "Just how many baby daddies does this woman have?" I had to bite my tongue more times than I care to admit, because I immediately wanted to defend my reputation by making sure the hearer knew these girls were being adopted. They had different names because I didn't give birth to them. It was someone else with all the baby daddies, not me. Internally I wanted to pass the blame on to their birth mother to save my own reputation.

I spent too much time during those early months fighting with my brain over this ridiculous behavior. Who cares what other people think? So what if they thought the worst of me? I know the truth. My husband knows the truth. My friends and family know the truth. It shouldn't matter what strangers think of me.

Luckily, those weird internal reactions faded after a few weeks and now seem like a distant memory.

This chapter just got too heavy. In the spirit of discussing my pre-teen daughters, I think it is time for a dance party or some cartwheels or a costume change. Go ahead and go crazy. I'll see you in the next chapter.

Chapter 4
The "infamous" Big and Little

My children have gained some notoriety on Facebook (among my friends, anyway) and some people follow me on social media just for the girls' hijinks. Both girls are pretty hilarious, but mostly they are hilarious without actually trying.

When the girls first came into our home, we couldn't post any specifics about them on social media due to confidentiality rules. You're not allowed to post pictures or identifying information on social media to protect the identity of foster children. So, I identified my girls only as "Big", meaning big sister, and "Little", meaning little sister. It became kind of a thing to post funny stories of our conversations or the funny ways one of them would misspeak.

Here's an example of the solid gold you might see from my children:

> Walking out of the bedroom behind Little –
>
> **Little:** Excuse me! [*Turning to look at her booty*] Stop it! No more farting!

Or this gem:

> Scripture, as read by Little –
> "Faith makes us sure of what we hope for and gives us proof of what we cannot see. Herpes 11:1"

Here's a few more:

Little: You know Barack Obama? Did you know he was the first man to ever be Black?

Little: Hey Mom, you know my nillicious?
Me: What?
Little: Nillicious!
Me: I don't know what that means. Do you mean like the book "Pinkalicious"?
Little: No. It's not a book. Nillicious....like A & M. Nillicious.
Me: Still don't get what you're saying. Do you mean "delicious"?
Little: NO! NILLICIOUS. NILLICIOUS....Like my name!
Me: ???
Little: You just don't get it! Like A & M in my name. NILLICIOUS.
Me: Ohhhhh........I think you mean INITIALS.
Little: Yeah! Nillicious!

Little: [*somersault*]
Little: [*karate chop*]
Little: [*bounce, bounce, bounce*]
Little: [*cheer kick*]
Little: [*jumping jack*]
Little: [*hop, hop, hop*]
Little: [*cartwheel*]
Me: Little isn't getting another soda until she turns 18.
Little: [*bounce, karate chop, dance, cheer kick*] What......I'm NOT hyper! [*jumping jack, cartwheel, hop*] I just need to move!
Me: Right.........not hyper......

Singing "Joy to the World" –

Little: ...and Mother and Nature sing, and Mother and Nature sing, and Mother and Mother and Nature sing...

Little: Watch this! I know a magic trick. [*Takes rock from her rock collection, hides in I'm her hand, places her hand behind her, raises one leg and pretends the rock came out if her butt*] Ta! Da!

Conversation in the car on the way home from Branson –

Big: What different kinds of milk are there?
Me: Whole, 2%, 1% and Skim
Big: Ewww! Gross!
Me: What's gross about skim milk. It's just fat free. Its the same stuff you drink at school.
Big: What?! We don't drink that at school! That's gross!
Me: What's gross about it being fat free.
Big: Yeah, but "skin"? Why do they call it that?
Husband: No...not "skin". It's SKIM....with an "M". Skim Milk.
Big: Oh...

Talking about voting –

Big: Did you vote for that one guy?
Me: Yes.
Little: I know a voting person. That Franken guy. Franken Opperbommer.
Husband: Who?
Little: His name is the same as Big's color.
Husband: Do you mean Black? His last name is Black?

Little: Yeah! That's it! Wait....his last name starts with an "O". Opperly....Opy....Oppen-bonner.
Husband: Wait.....OBAMA?! President OBAMA?! Is that who you are talking about?!
Me: His name isn't anything close to Franken Opperbonner!

While trying to concentrate on a movie —

Little: Blah, Blah, Blah
Husband: Shhhh...
Big: Talk, Talk, Talk
Me: Shhhhhh...
Little: Gab, Gab, Gab
Husband: SHHHHHHHHH!
Big: Mumble, Mumble, Mumble
Little: Argue, Argue, argue
Husband: WOULD YOU TWO JUST BE QUIET SO I CAN HEAR THIS!!!
Little: Is this almost over?
Husband: No.
Little: Good! Because I LOVE this movie!

Talking about the animal crackers in her lunch at school today —

Little: .....Yeah and there were these animals....well, not real animals.....and they were crackers....well, not actually crackers....and they were shaped like Smurfs, I think....well, not exactly like Smurfs.....well, maybe they were Smurfs.....or whatever...

Little: I'm a real Communist, aren't I?
Husband: What?!
Little: I make people laugh.
Husband: I think you mean "Comedian".
Me: Yeah…I'm not sure that Communists are especially funny.

I have hundreds of stories just like these.

Chapter 5
Ground Rules

A lesson in history or economics or psychology or something

Raising children is confusing, tough business, but raising former foster children adds a new level of strangeness to it. Since we don't have any biological children to compare them to, it is hard to know which behaviors are normal kid behaviors and which ones come from their "past lives".

I am using the plural "lives" very intentionally. My two children have lived three distinct lives: the first five-to-seven years under the care of drug-addicted parents who were neglecting their children; the second two-plus years bouncing around the foster care system; and the past few years as "our" children. Each phase of their life brought a different set of habits, some good and some not-so-good.

One behavior I think is a product of their past lives is the sense of entitlement and unhealthy expectations my children had when they first moved in with us. You might be reading that thinking "How can they have 'unhealthy expectations' living in a home that is so safe and provides them so much more than they had in the past?" That's the same thought we have had many, many times.

The interesting thing about kids raised in a welfare system is that they have sometimes been trained to expect things to come to them without any work. Their experience in the past may have taught them as much. Each month, without a job, my children's biological parents received enough money from the government to afford food to eat. Helping agencies gave them clothes for free and each year they got free school supplies. They likely received a generous free meal at Thanksgiving and free presents at Christmas. Other than cooking meth, their parents didn't have to lift a finger – and my children were raised seeing that lack of effort as the norm.

My children didn't have to take good care of the free items

they received because they knew that in a few months they'd get another round of free items to make up for the ones they broke or lost.

I have a friend who pointed this out very clearly. She lives in rural Alaska where residents receive an annual payout from the oil companies who are using their land for large profits.

For many Alaska residents, particularly those in poverty, they see their payout as more money than they've ever held in their hands at one time. They dream of all the things they've always wanted – that they can now afford with their new "wealth". Instead of seeing the payout as an investment to be used for paying off debt or to pay bills during the hard winter months, these newly-rich residents would splurge on a new boat or snow mobile or whatever they have "always" wanted to own.

But then a few months later you see the crashed, broken down, decaying "dream object" laying in ruin off to the side of their property. No big deal! The next payout will come along soon and the broken item can be replaced!

According to my Alaskan cousin, this pattern continues year after year. Each time she sees people go back to living in abject poverty because they used their temporary wealth to satisfy an itch, instead of using it as an investment to rise out of poverty.

For people in these situations (whether it be payouts from oil companies, the government, student loan disbursements, or aid from the local church) what matters most is what they can see in the moment – the here and now. On the day the check arrives they think "In this moment I have enough money for a vacation (or a flat screen TV or a new cell phone or...) so I will spend this money on the thing I've always dreamed about. Today is what matters because all I can see is this moment here, this choice now. The future has always been bleak and hopeless, but in this moment I can buy myself some happiness."

As I saw my children break their expensive toys or lose items out of carelessness I wondered: Is this "normal" kid behavior? Or is this the side-effect of poverty-induced entitlement? Do my children expect that I will just give them a new expensive toy or replace that lost item because that's what the government used to do when they were in poverty or in foster care? And, what is maybe worse, will they always expect that "real life" will work that way when they are adults?

My response has usually been to go the route of the "mean mom" by making them work to earn the money to replace their broken toys or lost items. The process of working to earn money to buy things is important training for my children whose earliest memories were of a more unhealthy way of caring for themselves.

Yeah, I know I'm a big meany-pants, but I really don't mind

It is funny how people give their opinion without really giving their opinion. Like when I mention a rule in my house and get a response like "You run a tight ship, Cap'n." What the person is saying in a playfully-sarcastic "I'm joking but I'm really not joking" way is that they think my rules are too strict.

However, when I get that response the person isn't usually looking at the full picture of my family situation. The reality for my family is that my children need boundaries. They crave boundaries. It isn't like they say "Golly gee willickers, Mom, I am sure glad you make me go to bed at 9:00 p.m. on a school night. I'm a happier child when I am well-rested."

No, we generally don't receive many verbal "thank you's" for our household rules. But my children certainly communicate their thanks through their behavior.

Also, as with so many things, it is important to understand the context of our particular family. Boundaries are important for all kids, but they are especially important for kids who have come through the foster care system. Their early life was unpredictable and many of the life events they have faced left them with fear, uncertainty, and insecurity.

Predictable routines and clear rules help children feel secure in knowing what will happen, when it will happen, and what the outcome will most likely be. Boundaries help my children feel confident that what happens today is going to be the same as what happened yesterday and the day before that. They don't have to spend their days and nights worried about the rug getting pulled out from under them like it did so many times in the past.

In our house, we have a very clear daily schedule that doesn't change much from one day to the next. Meals are served on pretty much the same schedule each day and so are snacks. My girls, who grew up in poverty and came to us with food insecurity, no longer have to worry about when they might see food again because they know meals happen on a reliable schedule. And I have a menu posted on the fridge telling them what we will be eating. This helps with budgeting and grocery shopping, but it also provides security. There are no questions driven by anxiety over food.

Other parts of the schedule help my children know what we expect — and what they need to do to meet our expectations. For example, homework happens reliably after they get off the bus and have a snack. We read for twenty minutes each school night and then do homework until all the homework is done.

The TV doesn't click on until all homework is finished by both girls, because a quiet house is good for concentration. We love letting the girls play with neighborhood friends, but they know homework is the first priority and must be finished before getting to play. Friends and TV provide important incentives to finish their responsibilities. It also reduces complaints, fighting, and frustration later in the evening due to stress. They take care of business early on and have lots of freedom with their time in the evening.

Similarly, we have chores scheduled into the week. Chores are an all-hands-on-deck activity. Having it as a regularly scheduled part of family life means that we hear almost no complaints or arguments during chore time. (Please note: this doesn't include daily chores like doing the dishes, cleaning up after dinner, caring for our dog, or taking out the trash when the can is overflowing — those things happen as needed and not just once/week).

In our family we believe in taking care of our home and keeping it nice. Each evening we pick up our belongings and put them away (or at least put them in our respective bedrooms until chore day). We have rules about certain activities that could damage walls, pictures, the carpet, furniture, etc. Lots of people have a philosophy that allows children to be children, even if a mess is left in their wake. My children are old enough to respect other people's belongings and to take responsibility for keeping things safe. Certainly we have fun at home, but they know which activities are off limits and what the consequences will be if rules are broken.

My husband and I take a long view of parenting. It is easy to see what a short view of parenting looks like. Just turn on most TV shows and you'll see fictional parents who have a short view of parenting their kids. Being friends with your kid, buying them whatever they want, making sure all gratification is instant, and letting kids behave disrespectfully are all great examples of short-view parenting.

I love my children, but I know that the world will not love them if they are rude, impatient or greedy. My children are always welcome in my home, but I do most-certainly hope they are able to live on their own as adults someday. What that means is that my children will need to be able to get a job, keep that job, manage their money, care for a home, and obey laws.

Toward that end, my children need to practice taking care of their belongings because those things cost money to buy and they cost money to fix or replace. We teach them to manage their allowance by teaching them to save a portion and to use a portion for offering at church. The money that is leftover is theirs to spend, but we encourage them to spend it wisely on things they really want, rather than whims and momentary fancies. And we don't buy them whatever they beg for, because that's not a reasonable standard to live up to. When they are adults, especially when they are just starting out on their own, they won't be able to afford to buy everything their hearts desire. Bills will come first and saving for a rainy day will be more important than constantly giving in to the latest whim.

Someday our children will be law-abiding citizens because they are learning yesterday, today and tomorrow to obey rules at home and at school. If they mess up at school we don't call the school to complain to the teacher. We talk to the teacher about what happened and how we can encourage our child to make better choices. When rules are broken at home, the consequences match the "crime" – because that is what happens in real life.

Someday my children will be able to care for their own home because we are already teaching them to do their own laundry, use a vacuum cleaner, clean the toilet, take out the trash, clean up food spills, and how to wash dishes.

Plus, my children need to practice using manners and respectful behavior toward others, especially authority figures. We have fun with our children, but they know very clearly that we aren't their friends.

If it seems like I run a tight ship, it's probably because I do. But I don't really care if you think it is too tight. My children's behavior tells me they feel loved and secure here. And, on rare occasions, they thank my husband and me for giving them a good place to live where they know it is safe – that's what tells me all our boundaries are worth the effort.

This is how we do it

Everything is harder when you are parenting kids who spent a large part of their life somewhere else. It requires long weeks and months (and maybe even years) to undo damage from someone else's lousy choices. And it requires a laser-focused commitment to providing consistent expectations and routines.

My girls came to us at ages ten and eight. They entered foster care at ages eight and almost-six. Their formative years were spent in poverty with parents who were using and producing methamphetamines in the trailer where they all lived. My girls share the same biological mother and they have two brothers who were not part of their foster placements. Little

Sister shares a biological father with one of her brothers and she was the apple of her father's eye. She was treated like the special one because she was wanted, unlike her siblings who were accidents produced from biological mom's other relationships.

Big Sister was the least wanted child in their family; her brown skin a constant reminder to everyone in the family that she was an accident from her mom's past. It was Big Sister who endured the most emotional and physical abuse, especially by Little Sister's dad.

They moved from one school district to another at the end of one school year and entered foster care shortly into the next school year. They changed foster placements four months later. That means they changed teachers three times in only six months. They remained in the second foster placement, which was a kinship or family placement, for one year and then moved to a third foster placement for their final six months before moving in with us.

If you had a hard time following all that, then you're almost ready to become a foster parent. For those of you who kept up with the previous paragraph, you might have noticed that the girls had four sets of "parents" across the span of just two years. That's a lot of transitions and loss to endure at such a young age.

They were lied to by their biological family and the rug was repeatedly pulled out from under them. Both girls entered our home excited about their new home, but only cautiously-optimistic that we would be different from everyone else in their lives. They expected us to disappoint them and be just as dishonest as everyone else. Every event was an opportunity to experience stress that things were different than they used to be. Needless to say, our job as parents was challenging in the beginning.

My husband and I made the decision to keep a very routine life in our home, with schedules that vary little from day to day.

Here's our typical school day schedule:

6:30 a.m.	Wake up, get dressed, eat breakfast, brush teeth, and gather school stuff
7:30 a.m.	Go to bus stop
3:45 p.m.	Come home from school, eat snack, read 20 minutes, and do homework
5:30 p.m.	Dinner as a family
7:30 p.m.	Shower, eat snack, spend time as a family
8:30 p.m.	Read a book or devotion and do bedtime prayers
9:00 p.m.	Bedtime smooches, hugs and lights out (bedtime has gotten later as they grew)

From the moment they wake up to the moment they go to bed, the routine is consistent and predictable. We have found that the predictable routine has given the girls a sense of safety and security they were missing in all the transitions and dysfunctions of their previous life. Plus, having a consistent routine reduces misbehavior because there are no surprises and they know how to meet our expectations.

Obviously, things come up that change the schedule sometimes. Sometimes we have church or school events that get us home too late to start the bedtime routine at 7:30 p.m. Or someone might invite us to dinner at a time other than 5:30 p.m. We are human like everyone else and are flexible to handle changes in the schedule when they come up. However, we usually talk about changes to the schedule up front so the girls aren't blindsided by them. That way they still know what to expect and they know they can trust us as we go with the flow together.

Weekend schedules are more relaxed and flexible, and bedtime is a little later. Behavior on weekends was always more challenging in those first months because the boundaries were less clear, which resulted in attempts to see how far we would bend. It took longer to establish positive weekend behavior due to this, but within six months we had a fairly good routine for those days, too.

Every family member is part of caring for our home

Another parenting decision that has been critically important relates to chores. We decided that chores would be an expectation for each girl, each week. Kids from dysfunctional homes often grow up without seeing good housekeeping habits or good standards of cleanliness. Without seeing parents regularly going to and from a stable job, kids might not understand positive work-related behaviors. It was important for us to provide habits with a lifelong benefit, like reading each night and doing chores.

Our way of doing chores is definitely not the only way to do it. I'll start by detailing our method and then give some other ideas.

Chores at our house are concentrated on Saturdays. Everyone jumps into action as we clean the house together. Each person has a set of responsibilities. The girls have a list that rotates between them so that it is fair. They're responsible for their own room, of course, and their own laundry. They put their laundry in the washing machine, switch the clean clothes to the dryer and put their own clothes away where they belong once they are clean. Chores they complete for the house include vacuuming the main living spaces, cleaning the bathrooms, and gathering the trash from everyone's trashcans. While they complete their chores, my husband and I also do our own set of household tasks.

The television stays off during chores, because we have found that it only slows down everyone's work as people stop to watch. We do, however, love to clean with upbeat music blasting throughout the house.

The girls have responsibilities during the week, too. They are responsible to clear the table after dinner, to put their own belongings away each evening, help with the dog, assist with groceries, and other tasks as they come up.

We do not pay children for chores. Our philosophy is that we all are part of the family and we all have a responsibility to make our household clean and comfortable.

We do, however, pay allowance separate from chores. My husband and I looked at several different allowance philosophies before we chose our method. We decided to give a set allowance that corresponds with the child's age. When our child was ten, she got ten dollars per month in allowance. From that ten dollars we took ten percent out and put it in a piggy bank that she can't open until she turns sixteen. Another ten percent is taken out and she uses that for offering at church. That means at age ten she walked away with eight dollars each month that was hers, free and clear, to spend or save as she pleased.

When the girls first came to live with us, every trip to the grocery store or mall was met with tears, begging, and whining for us to buy them every item they laid eyes on. It was painful taking them to Wal-mart or Target because they couldn't contain their disappointment over my unwillingness to give in to their every whim or immediately gratify their every desire. Allowance solved that shopping-drama as it let them buy those things for themselves. If they don't have money, they don't buy "on credit" with promises to pay us back after allowance day. Our mantra is "we don't buy things we can't afford".

We have found that using their own money to pay for things has decreased their whining at the store and has made them much more mindful of which things have real value. If it were our money to spend and they didn't feel the pain of it, they would want every item that looked sparkly, tasty, or adorable. When it is their own money at stake, those items look less tantalizing in comparison to the items they *really* want. Plus, when the girls save for large items (like a new iPod), they take much better care of their stuff than they do with items that didn't take so much effort to earn.

When the girls first joined our family, allowance was spent within hours of receiving it. The same happened with birthday or Christmas money. They would each immediately start begging, cajoling, and harassing us until we went to Wal-Mart or the mall. Money would fly out of their pockets for things that would last almost as long as it took to leave the store. Then their pockets would be empty and the rest of the month would stretch into infinity before the next allowance payday rolled around.

As the pattern continued month after month, we began having conversations about using their money in a different way; saving their money to buy things they really wanted, instead of watching their money flit away after whims. At first our parental wisdom fell on deaf ears. The flashy or tasty item was too attractive to their instant-gratification trained brains and they couldn't turn away.

Eventually, though, the promise of something bigger and better began to whisper in their ears. Our oldest daughter was the first to begin saving her money for larger items, which makes sense from a developmental standpoint.

After her younger sister saw the amazing purchasing power that her older sibling had amassed, both girls were on the savings bandwagon. In fact, our youngest daughter saved to such an extreme that she became almost unable to spend it when the time came to buy the thing she had been saving for! As she watched her money go into the cash register she became almost teary-eyed that all her hard work was going away in exchange for a thing – even though it was a thing she had been wanting for months. I chuckled inside as I watched her sweet lament and, to be totally honest, I had a mental dance party to celebrate my parenting win.

Other families use a variety of different chore and allowance methods, which are also very effective. I have several friends who pay allowance only for extra chores completed on top of regular family chores. For example, a child might have regular chores including pet care, cleaning their room, and dusting the furniture; but may earn allowance for mowing the lawn and washing the family car.

One family I know gives their child a fairly sizable allowance each month and the child uses their allowance for most of their own expenses, including: all snacks outside of the home, all toys (other than holidays), extra clothes, the child's own cell phone, and all outings with friends.

When we were researching different methods for managing chores and allowance, I searched the website Pinterest to find many great options. There were craft sticks with different chores written on them and children would pull several sticks each week and take care of those specific chores. I saw chore cards where kids earned a certain number of punches for each chore completed and after a set number of punches were earned they could "cash it in" for a reward. There were adorably-themed family chore centers with charts and reward stickers. Different systems may work for different ages.

Whichever system you choose, it is wise to consider some sort of chores for even small children. It is important to see their role within the family as something important and interconnected. Chores also provide good training for adult responsibilities.

Pleasant behavior leads to pleasant results

I was reminiscing recently about something from year one of foster-adopt life. That year we had a lot of tantrums, whining, lying to get out of trouble, arguing, and crying. Our quote during that year was "Pleasant behavior leads to pleasant results; unpleasant behavior leads to unpleasant results".

We talked to the girls about how that statement is true in our home and everywhere else. Unpleasant behavior hurts our friendships, causes people not to trust us, and it can cause us to get kicked off of teams or fired from a job. There are all kinds of unpleasant outcomes that the world will offer us when we make the wrong choices in life.

To help our girls have a visual of this concept, we posted a list of unpleasant and pleasant behaviors on our fridge where they could see it. When behaviors came up, we could refer to the list on the fridge as we quoted "Pleasant behavior leads to pleasant results; unpleasant behavior leads to unpleasant results". It became a mantra in our home that first year or so that the girls lived with us.

Here's the list we used based on what was happening in our home:

Unpleasant Behaviors
Whining
Tantrums
Crying to get out of trouble
Insults
Lying
Fighting
Arguing
Disrespectful tone of voice
Disobedience
Demanding
Selfishness
Getting angry when losing a game
Yelling
Slamming the door

Pleasant Behaviors
Asking nicely for what we want or need
Using "please" and "thank you"
Saying "I'm sorry"
Using "I" messages to express tough feelings
Obeying right away, all the way
Telling the truth
Crying only when hurt or sad
Solving conflict peacefully
Putting others first
Cooling off when angry
Accepting "no" as an answer
Staying calm when losing a game
Respectful tone of voice

When unpleasant behaviors happened, we could remind the girls of the list on the fridge. We reminded them an unpleasant result was coming if they continued in that behavior. Then we could direct them to choose one of the pleasant behaviors if they wanted a pleasant result.

It really did take about a year of often using our quote "Pleasant behavior leads to pleasant results; unpleasant behavior leads to unpleasant results", but we saw fewer and fewer unpleasant behaviors and more of the pleasant alternatives. They definitely aren't perfect, but this list allowed us to make incredible progress toward being respectful and kind. Regular tantrums are a distant memory in our home. Gone are the days when our children tried to get their needs met by demanding, whining and fighting.

Ours is certainly not the only discipline method to deal with unpleasant behaviors and not one that would work with every kid. There are some great systems out there. My favorites are: *Cognitive Discipline* by Dr. Becky Bailey, *Love and Logic* by Jim Fay and Foster W. Cline, M.D., and *1-2-3 Magic* by Thomas W. Phelan, Ph.D.

Many parents find behavioral reinforcement (a.k.a. sticker charts) effective to encourage positive behaviors. Other people prefer more of a deterrent method using things like lost privileges, time-outs, and the like. I've seen parents use all kinds of methods with great success.

The success of a discipline strategy depends largely on what speaks to a child's particular wiring – and, of course, on how consistently parents use that method. Nothing will undermine discipline with your foster-adopted child like being wishy-washy in how you apply and enforce the rules in your home. If I could point to the number one cause of discipline failures I've witnessed, it is inconsistency. Kids are like sharks sniffing out blood in the water. They see parental waffling as some sort of golden ticket to misbehave at will with no repercussions.

In case you wondered, the number two cause of discipline failures I have witnessed would have to be parents who repeatedly say they're going to do something and then never follow through. "If you do that one more time, I'm coming in there and you're gonna get it!" First of all, kids know that the word "it" means nothing in these scenarios. Second, they know you're busy surfing Pinterest or Facebook and don't want to come in there to give "it" to anybody. It's an empty threat.

When I was a kid in the 1980's, I knew my mom was busy drinking Tab and watching "Days of Our Lives" in the other room. However, experience had taught me that if she said I was "gonna get it" then she was definitely not above putting her Tab on a macramé coaster to come give "it" to me in a way I would really regret (like taking away my Atari for the rest of the week).

It was true in the 1980's and it is just as true now: when kids know you mean what you say, they'll trust you more and your discipline will be more effective. My mom may not have buckled us into car seats or made us wear helmets back then, but she did know something about discipline.

Santa Claus, Easter Bunny, and a clean conscience

Spoiler Alert: If you love Santa, the Easter Bunny, and all the other holiday "friends", you might want to skip to the next chapter.

Our girls were lied to by several adults in their early lives. They love us, but in the beginning they expected us to be liars, too. It took a very long time to earn their trust as much as we have, which probably isn't complete trust even now.

Because of their history, my husband and I decided to be 100% honest with the girls at all times, even if it is somewhat painful...even if it is unpopular. That made celebrating Santa Claus and the Easter bunny tricky business. While I know that most parents celebrate those traditions and feel no shame for such innocent white lies, we felt that even a little falsehood might erode the girls' confidence in what we say at other times. So, we decided not to actively encourage Santa or the Easter Bunny.

The trick to this choice was that our girls came to us believing in these magical holiday characters. They expected Santa to bring them presents and the Easter Bunny to bring them candy and toys. We didn't want to steal all their childhood joy, so we allowed them to believe. We let them put cookies out at Christmas when they asked to, but we (as parents) didn't write Santa's name on any presents or tell them Santa ate the cookies. We got baskets of treats for Easter, but we never once stated that the Easter Bunny had visited.

Eventually, they grew up enough to begin asking questions. When they asked us outright if Santa Claus was real, we started by putting the question back in their lap with, "What do you think?"

Eventually that wasn't enough of an answer so we made sure they genuinely wanted to know the truth before we dashed all their hopes and dreams for good.

In exchange for robbing them of their childhood (just kidding, it wasn't that dramatic...I just like to use hyperbole in my writing), we created other fun holiday traditions. For example, each Christmas we make a family Christmas movie. In one movie, we pretended that the Elf-on-a-Shelf came alive because the girls touched it and the real-life elf (played by my husband dressed in a goofy elf costume) was not happy. He was so frustrated by their disregard for the sacred Elf-on-a-Shelf rules, in fact, he wrote to Santa and told him to skip giving the girls a gift. They got to dramatically cry as they pretended to open a gift filled with coal. In another year's movie, we pretended that the girls were so engrossed in their handheld devices that Santa was able to come into the house, eat the cookies, play some video games, have a dance party, and take a nap: all without the girls taking notice. We've had so much fun with our "honest" traditions that the girls don't even miss the old ones.

Chapter 6
Making up for lost time

I have a mind full of memories from a stable childhood where I lived in the same home with the same parents and the same brother and went to the same school. My mom grew up in the town where we lived and most of her extended family still lives in the same area. My dad was an Army brat as a kid and decided to put down very permanent roots to make up for his young life spent moving every two years.

Most of the kids I started kindergarten with were there to walk across the stage at our high school graduation (even that one little jerk who kicked me under the table every time our kindergarten teacher had her back turned).

My brother and I have hundreds of shared stories from our lives and my whole family has a full arsenal of inside jokes from a lifetime creating memories together. Like the time my brother ran audio wires down the hall from his bedroom to a speaker he installed under my bed, all so that he could pretend to be the voice of God whispering to me at night. Or all those times he turned off the hot water heater a few minutes after I had gotten into the shower. Those were some great brother-sister memories for sure.

Even though I was the second born child and, therefore, my parents were too tired to take as many pictures of me as they did my older brother, I still have hundreds of photos of myself from the time I was in my mom's belly to the time I had dinner with my parents a couple of weeks ago. I can compare my baby pictures to those of my brother, my parents and even my cousins. I count myself lucky to have such a full knowledge of my family history, even including that one crazy cousin who did too many drugs during the 1960's and now disco dances in public places where no music is even playing.

My children came to me with a lot of stuff; more than the usual amount of stuff you'd expect of children living in foster care.

One thing they brought was a life book that their foster parents were required to keep during their time in state custody. The life book contained two baby pictures and a couple of other pictures of my youngest daughter with her biological parents. Her older sister has only a couple of photos of herself as a toddler, but no baby pictures. The rest of the photos in the life book were all taken after the girls entered foster care at ages eight and almost-six.

My children can't compare their baby photos to their parents' baby pictures or even to each other because they have so few pictures to use for comparison. The pictures they have are mostly grainy snapshots. The first professional photo either girl ever had taken was a school picture and we only have copies of the ones from after they entered foster care.

As for history, they have very little knowledge of their biological family and no inside stories or jokes to share from their early life. In fact, enough time has passed that they have very few memories at all of their lives before foster care. Sadly, the few things they remember are traumatic, like the hamster they used to have that died because their parents forgot to buy food.

My girls joined our family when they were eight and ten. Prior to that, their memories were filled with drug abuse, exposure to Rated-R horror films, poverty, inappropriate language, poor nutrition, and neglect. They have to live with the childhood memory of the police ripping them away from the only life they had ever known and being scrubbed down in an emergency room to remove the traces of meth exposure. These sweet girls have known what it feels like to bounce around the foster care system, each time being exposed to a mixture of good and bad memories, along with loss and disappointment.

One of the things that has been critically important for us as a family is to create as many great childhood memories as we possibly could and to document those in photos. I take pictures of everything and each year create a family yearbook to document the whole year. Some of our new memories involve activities that any child might enjoy, like first day of school pictures, new pajamas at Christmas, and birthday parties.

But, my husband and I have also worked hard to replace some of those childhood experiences that our girls never had. We can't go back and swaddle them or bond during breastfeeding. There will be no shared stories about first steps, first words, potty training accidents, or their first favorite foods. Instead, we try to create new special first memories, like the first time the girls got to stay in a hotel room, the first time they rode a roller coaster, or the first time they saw the ocean.

Side note: taking children to a hotel for the first time after growing up in poverty is pretty awesome. They went from thing to thing making declarations full of amazement: "Did you see this?! There are actually TOWELS in here! Do we get to use those are they just for looks?" or "Did you see the little bottles of shampoo and conditioner?! Those are SO COOL!" It wasn't even that great of a hotel room, but they couldn't hide their joy at all the things they had never experienced.

We also bond through fun activities like Mom School (see below), scavenger hunts, progressive parties, balloon rockets, art projects, laser mazes, field trips, dance parties, MadLibs, and many more adventures. On snow days during our first years with the girls, I scoured Pinterest for ideas of games, crafts, and activities. During the summers I always spend a lot of time making sure my children aren't sitting idly in front of the television, melting into the fabric of the sofa. That means we play games, do crafts, create science experiments, write and perform plays, and cook together.

I'm sure there are people who feel I do too much to entertain my children. But I'm not really entertaining them, I'm creating memories with them. I have years of memories to make up for with my children. My friends who are biological parents have snuggled their babies from their first moment on earth. They have kissed all the boo-boos, bonded over midnight feedings, shared first steps, first words, first birthdays, and every other "normal" childhood memory. I didn't have those luxuries with my children and I am left with a very limited amount of time to build a happy childhood for them to reminisce about.

Soon enough my children will be teenagers and won't want to spend time with my husband and me. Until then I am watching the grains of sand dribbling out of the hourglass as time slips away. I have precious little time to build positive childhood memories with them – memories that will hopefully bond us together like glue, even as their adolescent development is pulling them further away.

Mom School is exactly like Hogwarts only without literal magic or Voldemort

In my "regular" life I have always a full-time educator. My degree is in social work but I have spent about 90% of my career working in education settings. Because I feel so strongly about education, it is one of my biggest priorities in parenting. Many of the things we do at home have learning as a goal. My girls have both gotten the short end of the stick when it comes to early preparation for school success. But they are hard workers and enjoy school, so they have made huge progress in the last few years. One way we improve their chances at success is something we have lovingly named "Mom School".

Mom School is pretty much what it sounds like. It is school taught by dear old Mom, generally during any long breaks we have from school (spring break, Christmas break, summer break, and sometimes snow days).

Some of the things we cover in Mom School are very ho-hum and mundane, like math facts. In the past, I watched my children take three times as long on their homework as they should have, simply because they didn't have their math facts memorized. Plus, most of the problems they missed were from simple math errors. So, math facts were a biggie in the early days of Mom School. Sometimes it is math games, but sometimes we practice by worksheets and rote memorization. Sure it's a Snooze Fest, but it's also effective.

I also am a huge fan of writing and think that it is one of the most critical skills I was ever taught. I had some absolutely amazing junior high and high school teachers who taught me what I know about writing and it was the main thing that got me through college and graduate school. One of my Mom School goals has always been to give my girls a leg up on the writing process so that when they are required to write for "real" school, it will feel like second nature. In Mom School we have done persuasive (or opinion) writing, creative writing, research writing, and even some poetry. I try to make it interesting with topics they enjoy or with thought-provoking prompts.

It wouldn't be Mom School if there wasn't some reading. I have a long list of books I love and we have a library card. One summer we focused on the genre of mystery. We studied the parts of a mystery story and then identified those parts as we read together. In fact, our over-arching theme that summer for Mom School was Crime Scene Investigation. We did some science of CSI, like studying fingerprints and lifting prints off of glass. As the girls completed different assignments throughout Mom School that summer, they were rewarded with clues to our overall Mom School Mystery, which they had to work together to solve.

The first summer I did Mom School with the girls there was much wailing and gnashing of teeth. But, after we got started they realized that Mom School was usually pretty fun. Some days the girls even beg to do Mom School. It isn't exactly like Hogwarts, but Mom School is sometimes pretty magical.

Chapter 7
Ghost stories aren't just for Halloween

Ghosts. I didn't believe in them until I adopted. Now we have plenty of ghosts haunting our household. There are ghosts of biological family members, previous foster parents, ghosts of experiences past and even ghosts of their adoption expectations. The ghosts aren't always speaking out loud, but they are always lurking. We as parents are sometimes compared to them, our parenting choices are affected by them, the girls' behavior is often driven by them, and we sometimes feel like lashing out at them. And I suspect the ghosts will always be with us.

Something old, something new...
Adoption is super weird sometimes. Most days it is like normal parenting. Our children get up, go to school, come home and do homework. We eat as a family, watch a little TV, and then get everyone ready for bed. Our children occasionally fight with each other (and by occasionally I mean at least ten times a day). The issues that come up at our house are generally the same issues as all parents of tween sisters. In general, the past stays in the past.

But once in a while – usually when we least expect it – the past comes back in a flash. One day it was the photo of birth parents that one child has stuck in her homework folder at school. When going through her papers she came across it and said "Oh, hi there mommy! I love this picture...it's so pretty!" And that was the end of it. She stuck the picture back in her folder with the rest of her homework and the night moved on like nothing had ever happened.

Except that it did happen. And it was a strange reminder that these children are ours...sort of. Some days it feels like they are 100% ours, and some days it feels like we are just marking time until they are old enough to track down their "real" parents and go back to living their old life.

Playing the "Real Parents" card

Most of the time our adoption experience has been very smooth. When we took the foster parent and adoption classes, it was clear that kids in foster care sometimes carry big baggage with them. We learned about feces smearing, peeing into air vents, harming pets, and other stories that sounded more like a horror film than reality.

Our own experience with kids in the foster care system has been very low-key when compared to kids who smear poop on the walls. Instead of bodily fluid, we have dealt with more drama from emotional baggage. We've had our share of tantrums, defiance, manipulation, and just plain bratty behavior.

After the first year of foster-adoption we saw an end to most of the tantrums and a reduction in most of the other negative behaviors. Consistent routine, clear boundaries, social skills training, and relentlessly practicing new behaviors brought a miraculous end to the most onerous baggage from our children's past.

But all is not sparkly unicorns, warm kittens, and magical rainbows at our house. The biggest behavior we face is with manipulation whenever we say "no" to one particular child. Raised hearing only "yes" from her biological parents, our home is a constant source of disappointment. We don't allow sugar for every meal and snack. No one gets to watch TV or play on devices during every waking moment of the day. We're not into constant entertainment, constant spending, constant coddling, or constant gratification. We say "no" a lot at our house. And we require chores, homework, extra reading practice, and manners. It's a hard knocks life around here for sure. I'm pretty sure Annie was glad not to be adopted by us.

Because of all our "mean" parenting, our children have plenty of opportunities to practice handling disappointment and delaying gratification. Eventually I'm sure they will thank us, but for right now we compare very unfavorably to their biological parents when it comes to instant gratification. My youngest child was favored by her biological parents and was given most everything she wanted (usually to the detriment of her siblings' needs). To describe her as a little spoiled when she came to us would be an understatement. She has had the most difficulty with adjusting to life with us. And because of that, she has been the quickest to play the "Real Parent" card when difficulties arise. When we say "no" to something she really wants (like going to a sleepover at the home of someone we've never met) she becomes sullen, withdrawn, and suddenly focused on how much she misses her biological family. Occasionally she even utters the dreaded words "My 'REAL' parents would have let me!"

Luckily I don't need to be popular with my children to feel good about myself. Their heartbreak at not getting a smart phone during childhood (like "everyone" else) or not getting to go to every sleepover will not matter by the time they are adults. Someday they will grow up and, hopefully, be well-adjusted adults with healthy relationships and the ability to keep a job. And someday they will also realize there were reasons their "real" parents didn't exactly succeed at parenting. The "Real Parent" card will someday stop being a weapon in their arsenal, gone by the wayside just like tantrums.

As for now we do sometimes have successes, even on bad days. Once in a while our youngest child actually apologizes for being mad that we said "no" and that she knows we're just trying to keep her safe. Those are great days and make us feel a little like we might be doing something right. I'm sure she'll put us in our place tomorrow, but for today I'm going to bask in the post-apology glow and pretend that I'm not screwing my children up completely. At least not today.

Daddy Warbucks doesn't live here

One ghost we endured early on in adoption was the expectation game. When our children's previous foster parents and caseworker began talking to the girls about adoption, they worked through a conversation about what the girls wanted in adoptive parents. It was meant to make them excited about the adoption journey and more willing to accept that their new life was going to be positive.

An unintended side effect of those transition conversations was the unrealistic expectations that it set up as the girls began dreaming of their ideal new parents. It was like the girls expected adoption to be this grand thing that would erase all discomfort from their existence. "We'll never be bored!" "They will buy us whatever we want!" "We will always have fun!" "I will never be without what I want ever again!"

I don't know if they watched the musical "Annie" before moving in with us, but their behavior in the beginning was almost like they had watched Annie to take notes about what adoption *could* be. Unfortunately for them, my husband and I are no Daddy Warbucks. Even if we had a Daddy Warbucks budget (which we definitely don't), we don't abide by the "money can buy happiness" philosophy.

For the first year of adoption, my husband and I were losing the expectations game. We would plan something we thought would be fun to do as a family and would say something like "Tomorrow we're going to do something fun." The girls would launch into a guessing game to see if they could figure out what the fun thing was going to be. We were always the losers at that game because their guesses were always far more spectacular and outlandish than our lame-o plans. When we'd finally get around to telling them what the real plan was, they were usually disappointed that it wasn't any of the stuff they had guessed.

Here's a typical conversation from that dark era:

Little: Can I have chocolate milk with my lunch?
Me: I'm going to say "no" because we're doing something later and you might get a sweet then.
Big: What are we doing? Are we going to the water park?
Me: No.

Little: Are we going to have a sleepover?
Me: Are you crazy? No.
Big: Are you taking us to the theme park?
Me: Ummmm.....that's not it either.
Little: Then where are you taking us?
Me: I thought we'd go see a movie.
Little and Big: What?! Why are we doing THAT?!

After this typical conversation, whatever event we planned would be done begrudgingly by the girls, complaining through most of the event. Or, worse, they would do something to get in trouble so we couldn't go at all. We had quite a few fun plans dashed due to behavior meltdowns in those days.

Sometimes that first year brought the opposite problem. We would plan something fun and end up spending a lot of money in the process, and the girls would immediately start asking what we were doing next. If we didn't have some equally impressive plan to follow what we had just lavished upon them, they would descend into complaints again.

For example, one time we had a sleepover on a Friday night where we had done special crafts, had order-out pizza (a rare treat at our house), and for dessert we had ice cream sundaes with lots of toppings. The sleepover included lots of games I had made up and we had rented movies for the girls to watch. It was a really well-planned sleepover and all the girls had a blast. But, by Saturday after the sleepover friends had gone home, my girls began to ask what we were doing next. When the answer was something like "taking a nap", the complaints were loud and obnoxious.

In these you're-such-lame-parents moments, my husband and I would generally start singing Janet Jackson's "What Have You Done for Me Lately?" to the girls to drown out their complaints. The song was more for our own enjoyment as adults than it was for the girls' benefit. Sometimes your only parenting recourse is to sing 1980's and 1990's hits.

I am only half-joking when I refer to it as a "dark era". It really was parental self-esteem drought during that time period. We would plan something we thought would score us a win in the parenting column only to have it end with our children rending their garments and smearing their bodies in the ashes of their overly-dramatic broken dreams.

At one point I was so fed up with the complaints that we "never" do anything fun I took our wall calendar and filled it with all the kid-oriented things we had done for the past month. It was hard to ignore the visual display of how much fun we had provided them and how rude they had been to repay our parental awesomeness.

Eventually, the girls began to realize that it was their expectations to blame for their disappointment and not our level of fun. They began to accept that their Daddy Warbucks expectations were never going to be met in our home and it was better to simply enjoy the life they had, rather than complain about the way they thought it should be.

The ghost of biology

One ghost that will never be solved for our oldest daughter is the ghost of biology. She shares a biological mother with her sister, but has a different biological father. Her biological mom isn't even 100% certain which man is the father. The girls' caseworker couldn't track down any paternal relatives in my older daughter's case. While this made our case simpler in adoption court, it has made the emotional fallout more tricky.

The issue doesn't come up often and she rarely shows much outward emotion over it. However, one way it often comes up is who she looks like. Little Sister looks like her biological parents and other biological relatives. She has a good idea of how tall she will be because of that. But when we talk about Big Sister, the answers are not so clear. She doesn't look like any biological relatives she has ever met. Her face shape, nose, lips, skin, and hair look nothing like her biological mother. When Big Sister looks at pictures in her life book, she can glean no guesses about how she might look or how tall she might be when she grows up.

Additionally, when making family trees at school or when people ask the girls about their siblings, Little Sister knows the answer with certainty. There are no questions for her about which siblings are out in the world because she knows them and has their photos. Big Sister doesn't know if there are other half-siblings in the world that her biological father has produced. Unfortunately, she really has no way of ever finding out for sure who in the world might have her same lips or nose or hair.

Big Sister keeps her cards close to her chest, emotionally-speaking. I wonder how often she looks at other pretty brown-skinned girls and wonders if that's her sister or cousin. How often does she look at brown-skinned men and wonder if that's how her biological father might look. Does she internally grieve that she resembles no one in her known biological family or in her adoptive family? This is a ghost that requires some parental vigilance to build self-esteem wherever we can.

This is a common ghost for kids of adoption. It is common for kids to spend their lives with an eye out for people who look like them; always wondering if that's a sibling or cousin or parent. There's often a constant niggling at the back of their minds about why they do "this" or why they look like "that". Kids of adoption are plagued with wonder about which parent or grandparent had a particular good or bad characteristic that was passed down. While they may not verbalize it, you can bet they are thinking about it.

Sometimes it's a walk in the park, sometimes it's a slog through the mud

Our ghosts have been pretty harmless and not terribly persistent when they make an appearance. We have been very lucky or blessed or whatever you want to call it.

Sometimes the hardest ghosts to battle are the ones related to grief.

The stages of grief are said to be:

- ✓ Denial
- ✓ Anger
- ✓ Bargaining
- ✓ Depression
- ✓ Acceptance

These stages are listed as nice, neat bullet points but that doesn't mean it is a linear process. It might be comforting to imagine grief moves forward in a predictable way.
If it did, the story would go a little like this:

"Johnny came into foster care after his parents were arrested on drug charges. Little Johnny was shocked at first and couldn't believe that his parents had done anything wrong. In his new foster placement he spent the first week staring out the front window waiting for his mom and dad to pull up in their pick-up truck to take him home. He refused to take part in family activities because he had a 'real' family of his own whose return he believed was imminent.

"But, as the week turned into two weeks and the caseworker came back to check on him, Johnny started to become really withdrawn and angry. He didn't just avoid family activities; he was actively frustrated whenever the foster parents tried to include him. Anger was directed at everyone: foster parents, biological parents, his caseworker, teachers, and friends. There were three solid weeks of tantrums, name-calling, and angry outbursts over nearly everything that happened in Johnny's foster home. He was increasingly in more and more trouble as the angry outbursts hurt others or the foster parents' possessions in the home. He spent many of his waking moments sitting in time-out.

"After a while, Johnny saw that anger wasn't getting him anywhere and the caseworker still wasn't doing anything to let Johnny see his parents. He decided that he would promise his foster mother that he would start 'acting right' if she would take him to visit his biological parents. She tried to explain why he

couldn't visit his parents in jail, but Johnny didn't want to believe her. He tried a few other tactics to get her to give in, but she wouldn't budge.

"After a week of bargaining, Johnny realized nothing was going to bring his parents back. He stopped eating like he used to and constantly complained about being tired. He didn't even get much enjoyment out of watching his favorite TV shows anymore. Johnny's foster mom often caught him crying at night after he got tucked into bed.

"After two weeks of sadness, Johnny started to come around. His foster mother made Johnny his favorite snack and asked him to watch a movie with her. While they were watching, he scooted closer to her on the couch and eventually rested his head on her shoulder. He had accepted that he was part of their family, at least for now, and that maybe things weren't so bad after all."

Unfortunately, that story is purely fiction. For most people who go through loss, the five stages of grief are rarely so easy to spot. They don't move through grief in a consecutive succession from one step right into the other. You might see one stage in the morning and another in the afternoon, with normal behavior in between. Another might stick around at varying levels for months and might seem like it will never get resolved.

Some stages of grief will get revisited each time a child enters a new developmental stage. As they understand things in an increasingly complex way, their eyes will be opened to new aspects of what happened to bring them into foster care. This will bring grief in new and unexpected ways.

Here is what the stages of grief have looked like in our house with Little Sister, who has shown the most obvious grief of my two girls:

Denial – As with all the stages of grief, one of my children has struggled more with denial than the other. We often revisit denial with her as she tries to convince herself and us that her biological parents didn't actually do anything wrong. She was an almost-six year old when she was removed from their home and had a child's innocent view of some of the ways her parents were failing at providing a safe, healthy home. We don't want to crush her view of her parents or to see us as against them, but sometimes we have to answer her denial statements with a few facts. For example, one day she was talking about how her parents didn't really do anything wrong, they just got arrested because someone "tattled" on them to the police. It seemed unhealthy to let her believe that people could face jail time in such a willy-nilly fashion. Our simple message to her in childhood is that actions have consequences and the consequence of breaking the law is going to jail. Her parents broke the law and that's why they went to jail. Their good intentions or love for her or her love for them doesn't change their unlawful choices.

Anger – The most onerous stage of grief is often the anger stage. We've definitely had our share of grief that has come out as angry outbursts, tantrums, arguing, disobedience, and fighting. But I have a background in mental health issues and can usually spot grief for what it is. When we have an outburst of negative behavior that looks a little like the anger from grief, we talk about it and our girls are usually able to recognize and verbalize their grief in those moments. This stage of grief comes and goes. Sometimes we have pleasant, enjoyable behavior and then, like whiplash, anger strikes when we least expect it. The root is some memory that has arisen and she either doesn't know how to express her anger at her parents for their bad choices or anger at us for taking her parents' place. Sometimes she is angry at the circumstances, other times she is angry at the outcome of her circumstances (like missing other loved ones who she left behind in all her moves). Her anger sometimes looks like plain old defiance that any child may show, but the root is often that we are asking her to do something that reminds her of some loss from the past. Note: This is different than other moments of anger that have a different trigger.

Bargaining – This is a stage that hasn't shown itself often in our house. Once in a while we get requests to visit biological relatives or questions about when we will allow contact with a biological parent. In the past, these requests most often happened in periods when anger or sadness was hanging over the house like a dark cloud. It's like seeing the biological relative (or even the promise to see them) seems to our hurting child to be salve for her inner wounds. What she doesn't realize is that actual contact would have created more wounds and made her sorrow even deeper than it already was. As time has gone on, we began to see fewer and fewer incidents of bargaining. Instead, when the topic of contacting biological relatives arises now, it involves more calm conversations about the choices she might make as an adult to reconnect with her biological family members and how that might feel.

Depression – Depression in children often looks very different than it does in adults. According to the American Academy of Child and Adolescent Psychiatry, here are some symptoms common to children and teens:

- Frequent sadness, tearfulness, crying
- Decreased interest in activities; or inability to enjoy previously favorite activities
- Hopelessness
- Persistent boredom; low energy
- Social isolation, poor communication
- Low self-esteem and guilt
- Extreme sensitivity to rejection or failure
- Increased irritability, anger, or hostility
- Difficulty with relationships
- Frequent complaints of physical illnesses such as headaches and stomachaches

- Frequent absences from school or poor performance in school
- Poor concentration
- A major change in eating and/or sleeping patterns
- Talk of or efforts to run away from home
- Thoughts or expressions of suicide or self-destructive behavior

We experienced several of these at different points, but not a persistent period that warranted treatment with medication. If your child displays one or more of these symptoms on a persistent basis and it interferes with his or her ability to function at school and other settings, it may be time to seek treatment. If you don't have a caseworker, then your pediatrician is a good place to start to get a reference for a psychologist or therapist who works with children or adolescents. A psychiatrist may be needed if treatment will require ongoing medication.

Acceptance – Luckily for us we live in the state of acceptance *most of the time*. Acceptance is where a child accepts the situation and they live life fully into that new reality. It doesn't mean they don't still think of the past or wish things had gone differently. However, when they think back on it during acceptance they realize that the past is something that can't be changed and that life is going to be okay moving forward.

While we enjoy the "final" stage of grief most of the time, we don't ever rely on it being our reality 100% of the time. The other stages still rear their ugly head from time to time. Periods of development are big triggers and so is stress. We still get periodic regression and we see grief cycle through for a day or a week at a time depending on what is happening. As she understands the past in a new, more mature way, new thoughts get triggered that cause her to revisit her feelings of pain again. It isn't always terrible and, as she has grown up, she has become more able to talk instead of lashing out.

The Ghosts that haunt indefinitely

I wish I could say that once grief is resolved and kids reach acceptance that everything will be hunky-dory. Unfortunately, the wounds from the past and the unlucky lottery of genetics sometimes leave kids with scars in the form of mental illness. Just like the little piggies going to market, some foster kids will have mental illness, some kids will have none. Some kids will get more than one diagnosis. According to the American Psychiatric Association, here are a few descriptions of mental illness you might see in a traumatized child or teen:

- ✓ **Post-Traumatic Stress Disorder (P.T.S.D.)** – This is a diagnosis for kids who have been traumatized by something, like abuse they have endured or witnessing something terrible that a parent has done (or had done to them). It can come with recurrent thoughts, nightmares, flashbacks, fear/avoidance of things that remind them of the trauma, and even hallucinations. They may have difficulty with sleep, irritability and outbursts of anger, trouble concentrating, and may easily startle. For example, I worked with a preschooler once who had witnessed his father being shot and killed. This little tyke wore a constant expression of exhaustion and anger and I don't remember ever seeing him smile. When naptime rolled around on days when he suffered nightmares and flashbacks, teachers and helpers took turns trying to comfort him as he sobbed and screamed. His cries were desperately full of anguish and pain, as if he were right in the middle of his father's murder scene again.
- ✓ **Oppositional Defiant Disorder (O.D.D.)** – A child with O.D.D. is going to have a long-lasting pattern of negative, hostile and defiant behaviors. It might include a quick temper, arguing with adults, actively refusing to comply with adult requests, deliberately annoying others, blaming others, being easily annoyed by others, and seeking revenge.

- ✓ **Conduct Disorder** – This is the mean older brother of O.D.D. Where the child with Oppositional Defiant Disorder often chooses to disobey authority figures, the child or teen with Conduct Disorder actively looks for ways to show aggression to people and animals, destroy property, be actively deceitful, and pursue serious violation of rules such as stealing and running away. A child with Conduct Disorder has very little regard for the rights or feelings of others and is not bothered by behavior that violates basic societal expectations. This diagnosis goes beyond normal teenage rebellion and leads to significant problems across a variety of life settings (school, employment, home, friendships, and legal).
- ✓ **Reactive Attachment Disorder (R.A.D.)** – This is a challenging diagnosis in adoption. Children who struggle to attach to their caregiver may not respond to social interactions or affection and may be ambivalent toward caregiver attention. But they may use a caregiver's desire for interaction as a manipulative tool to get what the child wants, such as showing much-wanted affection to the adult in exchange for a toy or candy the child may want. Alternately, a child with R.A.D. might show attachment with too many adults, showing intimate parent-child affection to all adults they interact with, including babysitters and teachers.
- ✓ **Depression** – Depression in children and teens is slightly different from that of adults. It can include **frequent sadness, tearfulness, crying along with decreased interest in activities;** or inability to enjoy previously favorite activities. Kids with depression might feel hopeless, have low energy and low self-esteem, struggle with guilt, rejection and failure, and difficulty with relationships. They may express their depression as irritability or anger or depression may come out as physical complaints like headaches and stomachaches. Some children and teens will become suicidal or will express suicidal ideas. I once worked in a group home with a seven-year old who was diagnosed with depression. He and his siblings had entered the foster care system under traumatic circumstances but he,

the youngest sibling, had the deepest wounds from the past. He was a dark, sullen child who didn't enjoy others and rarely played. After weeks of listless, withdrawn behavior, he attempted to physically harm himself and staff at the group home had to restrain him to keep him from doing further damage. Before that encounter I never dreamed that such young children could be suicidal. I was proven wrong and that experience has taught me to be careful in listening to what children say with their actions and words. Note: If a child in your care expresses suicidal ideas or plans, take action *immediately*. The number for the National Suicide Prevention Lifeline is: 1-800-273-8255.

- ✓ **Anxiety** – This is a common outcome for kids who have experienced trauma, such as removal from their biological home, abuse, neglect, and the ongoing trauma of bouncing around foster care. These kids are justified in their fears that the trauma may happen again or fear that other adults will repeat the unpleasant past. However, anxiety becomes a problem when it doesn't resolve and begins interfering with life functions, like school or friendships. Anxiety disorders in kids can be generalized anxiety (symptoms can show up in response to lots of different triggers, not just triggers you would expect given their past), separation anxiety, social anxiety, panic attacks, and may even have obsessive-compulsive characteristics. Our youngest child struggled with social anxiety for several years. She was a naturally shy child when meeting new people or entering new situations, but crossed the line into anxiety because she was selectively mute at school or other situations where she felt uncomfortable.
- ✓ **Attention Deficit Disorder/Attention Deficit Hyperactivity Disorder (A.D.D./A.D.H.D.)** – Some say A.D.D./A.D.H.D. is a product of nature (like many other illnesses and disorders are passed from parent to child). Others argue it is nurture (a product of the child's upbringing and environment). I would say it is a combination. For some children with a dysfunctional background, A.D.D./A.D.H.D. symptoms can partly be an

outcome of years of raising themselves with very few standards. They aren't accustomed to sitting quietly, focusing on boring tasks, and organizing their belongings. Those habits had no chance to attach to their young brains because it simply wasn't part of their experience. Instead, the opposite kind of habits were allowed to flourish. These kids were often raised by television sets or video games, which provide fast-paced, constant stimulation. Quiet activities aren't stimulating enough to hold their attention. They might be a disorganized mess because they lived in a home where trash and animal feces were literally covering every surface. There simply is no picture in their young minds of what tidy belongings ought to resemble. Other kids have A.D.D./A.D.H.D. because their biological parent or parents has it too (which might have led to adult self-medicating behaviors, such as drug abuse). Plus, research shows that prenatal exposure to alcohol and drugs results in a higher incidence of A.D.D./A.D.H.D. in children (see next point).

✓ **Fetal Alcohol Spectrum Disorder (F.A.S.D.)** – This one is just like it sounds, although instead of a mental illness it is more of a developmental disability. Aside from a few physical characteristics that are often common to kids with F.A.S.D. (such as narrow eye openings and smooth upper lip), there are several learning issues to note. Difficulty paying attention, learning and remembering, following directions, socializing, communicating, and controlling impulses are hallmarks of F.A.S.D., along with difficulties in physical coordination. As children and teens, kids with F.A.S.D. may make poor decisions, trust the wrong people, and make the same mistakes over and over again. Many of these behaviors look like A.D.D./A.D.H.D., but have their root in prenatal exposure to alcohol. Research points to the same kind of difficulties with exposure to illegal drugs.

The problem with these ghosts is that we can't usually tackle them on our own. Certain parenting strategies will help minimize the behaviors associated with these mental illnesses, but just loving our kids and providing a nice home will not erase all the damage. You will need help from a professional (or several) to make a dent in these diagnoses.

Tough conversations

All parents occasionally have tough conversations with their children. You might have to tell your kids about why Mr. Fluffernutter the gerbil has been napping for three days straight. Or that awful conversation when puberty begins and you have to initiate "the talk".

As adoptive parents, we have all those tough conversations just like "regular" parents. But, adoption brings a different kind of tough conversation.

More than once we have had difficult conversations about the poor choices made by our children's biological parents. It isn't always easy to balance the truth with what our children can handle hearing at their age. The questions they ask don't always need the entire truth – not until they are older and can grasp the complexity of what really happened.

Sometimes we can't avoid the tough conversations and we have to give 100% of the truth. One time, we had a discussion about why our younger child has an easier time with reading and spelling than our older child. The gist of the conversation was that Little Sister thought she was smarter than Big Sister and Big Sister confessed her belief that she isn't smart. Because of the unhealthy attitudes they were both expressing, we knew it was a conversation we had to have with some of the ugly details. We had to tell both girls the truth about their early start to school.

Big Sister was eight years old when the girls entered foster care. She had never attended preschool before starting kindergarten as a barely-five year old (she has a summer birthday and almost didn't meet the age requirement to enter kindergarten that year). With neglectful, addicted parents and a less-than-stellar attendance record, that first year of school was an abysmal failure. She repeated kindergarten with greater success the second time. She continued to live with neglectful parents and a dysfunctional, unpredictable existence until the start of second grade. Her second grade year began traumatically, with law enforcement forcefully removing the children from their meth-lab home. They bounced to a couple of different foster homes during that first semester of school. It was a terrible time in her life. Needless to say, her formative years of phonics instruction were less-than-ideal.

Little Sister, however, had begun kindergarten just three weeks before she entered foster care. Prior to that she had been in preschool. The transitions in foster care weren't ideal for her, but she definitely had a more solid foundation for learning than her sister had. Little Sister's learning was less interrupted by all the trauma. Her phonics instruction was much more successful – which is reflected in her higher reading and spelling ability now, several years later.

It was important to explain some of the details to our children and to discuss how that has affected both of them. Neither of them are responsible for the rocky start they had in life, even though they are both affected by the hard work required to overcome that rocky start. It would be impossible to gloss over the past when we talk about their current struggles.

In a way, though, the conversation freed them from some of their own assumptions about themselves. My oldest child knows she got the short end of the stick for the first eight years of her life and that she will be playing catch-up for a long time. But, knowing the truth also frees her from feeling inadequate. Her struggles are because of someone else's mistakes, not because her brain isn't smart enough.

My youngest child is also freed from feelings of inadequacy for some of her struggles. She, too, can look at her parents' poor choices as the source of some of her learning challenges.

Sometimes tough conversations are more painful, like when a child defends someone in the biological family who did something abusive or dangerous. Or when the biological parent has a mental illness and the child begins showing signs of the same diagnosis. Or when your child finds out his or her biological parent willingly stopped fighting for custody. Those conversations leave a bigger mark on the child's heart and are trickier to navigate without anger directed at the bearer of the bad news. These kind of especially-painful details should be delivered with the help of a child's therapist, if possible.

When we first brought our girls home, we weren't sure when the time would be right to have some of those difficult conversations about the past. I mean, how do you initiate that conversation without being super awkward?

The girls' therapist assured us that children usually let adults know when they're ready to hear the truth. She promised us that they would ask questions directly about their past when they were emotionally-ready to begin hearing about it. And she was right. Our fears have been relieved as time has moved forward with our girls. They bring up conversations when they have questions or when a memory pops up with its troublesome feelings. We answer their questions as honestly as possible, while protecting what we can of their feelings about their biological connection to the past.

I am sure we still have many hard conversations in our future. I don't look forward to those talks, but I no longer fear them like I did as a new adoptive parent. The girls will "tell" us when they are ready to hear the full story – and I am confident that we will be ready (with our therapist's help, if needed) to tell them.

Phones, social media and adoptive parent fears

One of my daughters recently received her first phone. She was thrilled to finally join the "club" like her peers. But the decision to enter the personal cell phone age has been fraught with trepidation for my husband and me. "Will she call her biological relatives?" "What if she calls someone from her past and tells them where we live?" "What do we do if she starts talking to her biological family and wants to visit them?" "What if she gets mad at us and calls them so she can run away to live with them again?"

Our fears aren't completely unfounded since many adopted children seek out their biological family members in adulthood. Social media makes that process easier than ever.

It is easy for me to look at their old life and see that they've got it a lot better now. Our home is safe and clean with plenty of yummy, healthy food to eat. They have their own rooms with lots of toys, clothes, shoes, books, art supplies, and other stuff that is just their own. Our children no longer worry about their school attendance or having someone to help with homework. They haven't had head lice since living in our home and they are given whatever medical care is needed, right away. On paper we are already way ahead of their biological parents on all those counts.

Plus, we provide lots of fun opportunities for our kids. They've travelled to a dozen different states in the four years we've had them. We've introduced them to water parks, roller coasters, museums, and the ocean – all things they had never experienced before.

When it comes down to it, however, we have one thing that their biological parents can give them, and that's biology. There's a deep-seated connection to those biological relatives that we can never give them. At some point our children will hunger to hear about their birth, their first words, and how they took their first steps. They'll want to know about their grandparents, aunts, uncles and cousins. If nothing else, they will want closure on why their biological parents signed the adoption papers instead of fighting to bring their children home.

Now is the time to make peace with the eventuality that our girls will seek out their biological parents. Who knows what that will look like? I suspect they will track them down someday and will have a sort of friendly relationship with their biological parents, rather than a parental one. And that will probably be okay. Someday that's a bridge we will surely cross.

Until then I will treat them as *my* daughters and continue to build a life with them that will be hard to deny. And when the time comes, I will try and make a bridge so they can safely pursue contact with their biological family without burning any relationships in their new life. It doesn't have to be "us vs. them" in their view of family relationships – it can be "us includes them".

Things in this chapter got really heavy. I think it is time for a few more quotes from my children.

Chapter 8
More "infamous" Big and Little

Little: [*emerging from the bathroom after a long day spent mostly outside*] Why is my face this color?!
Me: It's a sunburn.
Little: How is it a sunburn?
Me: Ummmm...because you've been in the sun most of the day?
Little: But how did that cause a sunburn?
Me: It is called a SUN-burn.
Little: Oh....I thought you only got those when you go swimming.

Talking about school lunch –

Little: [*reading from the school menu on the fridge*] Ugh....POPCORN chicken! Gross! I'm definitely taking lunch box tomorrow!
Me: You do realize "popcorn chicken" doesn't contain any popcorn. It's basically chicken nuggets that are the size of popcorn.
Little: Ohhhh....

Husband took Little shopping for a gift for Big's birthday. Little kept pointing out things that she loved, but Big would hate. Here's the conversation that followed –

Little: [*pointing to a glittery butterfly-shaped pillow*] Big would LOVE this! It's PERFECT!
Husband: No. She would NOT love that. There is nothing about that pillow that says: "Big would love this."
Little: I think it's perfect.
Husband: She would hate it.

Little: Yeah, but if she got it and hated it, then she would give it to me!

You've got to give her props for her savvy business sense, even if she doesn't score any points for thoughtfulness.

Sometimes dinner conversation spirals into strangeness –

Little: What do you want for your birthday?
Big: Oh, no...I'm not telling you. You can't get me the thing I really want – it's too much money.
Little: Fine. I'll get you bubbles.
Big: I don't want bubbles. That's weird.
Little: I like bubbles! Fine. I'll get you a necklace with a puppy or kitty on it.
Big: [*silent, but giving the "Are you clinically insane?" look to her sister*]
Me: You are only naming gifts *you* would want.
Husband: Yeah, it isn't *your* birthday yet. We're talking about what your sister would want.
Little: What?! I would give her a kitty necklace. Kitties are 'dorable!
Me: It's a good thing you aren't Santa Claus, because you are a terrible gift giver. "And here's a puppy necklace for little Jimmy, and a kitty necklace for little Johnny..."
Little: I would make a GREAT Santa Claus! I could get a reindeer and teach it how to let people ride it so that I could ride it...
Husband: ...and you wouldn't need much room for presents because kitty and puppy necklaces don't take up much space...
Little: And I could eat all the cookies. That would be DELICIOUS!
Me: Yeah, and you'd weigh a thousand pounds if you ate all those cookies! [*turning to Husband*] By the way, how does Santa not have diabetes?

Little: [*wheels turning as she solves a serious problem with her eat-all-the-cookies plan*] I could eat the cookies...I'd just have to stop and poop sometimes.
Me: Like at all the kids' houses? You're going to stop and poop at their houses while you're delivering presents? That's your plan?
Little: Well, not at EVERY house. Obviously.

Little: I know what [Friend] wants for her birthday. She wants the "Ever High" Barbie.
Me: So the Barbie who is on drugs?
Little: Huh?
Husband: I think you mean "Ever After High".

Little: [*singing*] I have a big butt and I cannot lie...
Me: Um...that's not quite how it goes.
Little: Yeah [*pause for dramatic eye roll*] it is...
Me: Whatever you say.

Chapter 9
Don't drink the Kool-Aid

When people use the phrase "Don't drink the Kool-Aid" they generally mean something like "don't be fooled" by a particular person or situation. Don't fall for their trap. It is a phrase that goes back to Jim Jones and the cult members he poisoned in 1978 with cyanide mixed into Flavor Aid (which was just like Kool-Aid, but with less cool marketing).

We use that phrase around here because we have recently discovered that artificial food dye was to blame for behavior problems in Little Sister. Over the years with her, we have endured many tantrums, angry outbursts, acts of defiance, and backtalk. At first, we thought it was due to being spoiled by her biological parents. They gave her whatever she wanted and never told her "no". In fact, they would often make her older sister give up what she had so that Little Sister would not be upset.

But, after years of consistent behavior training and consequences for these behaviors, we saw only slight improvement. Sometimes things would be great and then her behavior would take a downhill turn as though someone flipped a switch. It was like Jekyll and Hyde. Her behavioral whiplash was as mysterious as it was unpleasant.

At times we blamed her outbursts on the anger stage of grief, but it was too haphazard to fit that pattern.

She has a diagnosis of Attention Deficit Hyperactivity Disorder (A.D.H.D.) and fits absolutely all of the criteria as though the researchers were specifically writing about her. We made the decision to put her on medication to allow her to focus and to give her some control over her own feelings of out-of-control energy. But, the A.D.H.D. medicine didn't do anything for mysterious appearances of Rage Girl.

Then a miracle happened. A friend of mine, whose daughter is like Little Sister, mentioned that her child's behavior improved significantly when they eliminated artificial food dyes from her diet. Red 40, Yellow 5 and Yellow 6 were big culprits in triggering her daughter's negative behavior. I decided to try an elimination diet of my own and it was a game-changer. On days when she has no artificial dyes in her food, behavior is lovely, sweet, helpful, and she is able to accept change without much fuss. If food dye slips into the mix (as it did one day recently in the ice cream shop) Rage Girl makes a return and it doesn't take much for her to snap over the smallest frustration.

Since then, we have invested some time and effort into weeding out food dyes from our home and replacing those products with dye-free or natural dye. Aldi, an inexpensive chain of grocery stores, has committed to removing artificial ingredients from their products and we have found they have the largest selection of snacks, drinks, cereals, and candy of any place we have tried (other than their sister grocery chain, Trader Joe's).

Everyone in our family has noticed the positive change in behavior and has happily jumped on board the dye-free train to support Little Sister.

My friend and I aren't the only parents who have noticed the negative influence of Red 40, Yellow 5 and Yellow 6 on behavior. European countries ban those dyes from their food products, in fact. Google "food dye and behavior" and you'll find a plethora of articles on the subject. The research I tracked down using a double blind study didn't show a significant effect. However, my own anecdotal "research" has turned up several friends with foster or adopted kids who have tried food dye elimination with great success.

Eliminating food dyes isn't a magic bullet because not all children are sensitive to their effects. But, if you end up with a child whose behavior quickly swings from one end of the spectrum to the other and you notice the change happens shortly after a snack or meal, food dye elimination might be worth trying.

On a related note: Settling on an A.D.H.D. medicine isn't as easy as it looks on TV. You may go through several different kinds of medicine at different doses before you find one that works for your child. It may cause stomach pain, loss of appetite, weight loss, changes in mood, changes in personality, or other side effects along the way. Be prepared to spend a lot of time with your child's doctor or psychiatrist before you get it right and even then it might not be perfect.

Chapter 10
A cabinet full of hair products

For those of you who are African American, bi-racial, or just have naturally curly hair, you might want to skip this chapter – unless you just want a good laugh over my naivete.

I think I should start by telling you that I am a pale-skinned, Caucasian woman with stick-straight auburn hair. When I look back on the history of my hair, two memories stand out.

The first memory is my kindergarten graduation. I was a wee-tiny five-year old with hair that was long enough to reach my butt. My mom wanted me to have pretty curls for my big moment on stage, so that morning she washed my hair and put it into curlers. I spend the entire day with those curlers in my hair waiting for it to dry, which meant I had to be careful not to touch my hair. When evening came, my mom got me dressed in my best outfit and finally took the curlers out of my hair. It was the best my hair had looked in all my five years of life. Unfortunately, gravity, Missouri humidity, and my hair's stubborn nature were working against my beautiful curls. Within thirty minutes of taking the curlers out, my hair was back to stick-straight.

My other memory of having curly hair came in 1989. That was the year I paid $80 and spent four hours in a hair salon getting a spiral perm. For those of you too young to remember the 1980's and 1990's, we spent a lot of those years looking like we were in the band "Skid Row". That perm was glorious. For the first time in my life I had hair that was full of body and life. My bangs had never been so easy to tease and I was able to maintain four to five inches of height on my bangs with only half a bottle of Aqua Net. Those were the glory days for sure.

But, those two exceptionally-lame curly hair experiences did not adequately prepare me for dealing with my bi-racial child's curls. She has Type 3C curly hair, meaning that she has soft, corkscrew curls (Google "curly hair types" for more details).

While her hair naturally looks a little like my 1989 spiral perm, the texture and quantity of her hair is vastly different from mine. Even when my perm was in its finest Skid Row glory, I didn't need any extra products to keep my hair healthy and hydrated. I used the same shampoo, conditioner and Aqua Net I had always used and the results were just fine.

Curls, curls and more curls

My daughter's hair is not that simple. I knew we were walking into a different kind of hair care when we brought her home, but I wasn't expecting to have a cabinet full of hair products and I wasn't expecting to spend quite so much money trying to keep her hair healthy. There are conditioners (which are alcohol- and sulfate-free, of course), oils, lotions, curl revitalizers, and styling products to hold the curls in place or reduce frizz. But, not all products work nicely on my girl's hair, so we have products in the cabinet that were purchased and later abandoned. Most hair products smell great, but I have inadvertently purchased a few that smell like an old lady. We have a few stinkers lingering in our hair product graveyard along with the products that didn't work as promised.

Here's what we generally have found to work for our curly girl.

- ❏ She shampoos her hair only once or twice per week (twice if she's been especially active and sweaty), the rest of the days she co-washes, meaning she uses conditioner in place of shampoo. If she had Type 4 hair, she would shampoo more like every five to seven days.
- ❏ She uses oil and/or hair lotion after she has towel-dried her hair (both if her hair is especially dry).
- ❏ In the morning, she wets her hair (sometimes with water, sometimes with curl activator spray) and puts on more hair lotion to manage some of the frizz.

❑ If she is wearing her hair down, she uses either a spray or lotion-type styling product meant to define curls, but we avoid products that contain alcohol because they dry her curls out and create more frizz.

When the girls first came home, I did a lot of Internet research on her hair and asked friends what they used. Luckily, I have a dear friend who is a stylist and has her own curly hair to deal with. I also did a lot of research on styling curly hair. I didn't think my then ten-year old would appreciate looking like she had just fallen out of a late 1980's hair band, so my previous experience with curly hair was no help. The Internet provided a wealth of ideas. After a while, she learned what she liked and started to fix her own hair, first with a little guidance and then on her own. She still occasionally lets me fix her hair, even though she is now a full-fledged teenager. Those are great mother-daughter bonding moments that I cherish.

Ashy skin
I grew up in rural Missouri in a town that could only use the word "diversity" when talking about our shades of white, pink, or tan skin. I was probably the most diverse member of my class since I had pale white skin in an era where girls were slathering themselves with suntan lotion to get deep, dark skin so popular in the late 1980's and early 1990's when we didn't know so much about skin cancer.

It wasn't until I was an adult that I learned about ashy skin. This isn't a term Caucasian folks use when our skin is dry. Even when my skin is a little dry in winter, I rarely worry about how it looks to others because they won't likely notice. But, ashy skin is a really big part of African American hygiene. It is important for brown-skinned kids to use lotion because dry skin makes them look a little grey or even dirty. Lotion keeps the skin looking healthy.

We like lotions that don't have a smell. Since we use yummy-smelling hair products, we don't want the skin products to compete with that scent or even be too strong. Big Sister has a large bottle of lotion and uses it after she showers at night and again in the morning before she gets dressed.

Sunscreen is for everyone

I have pale skin and have always followed a pretty strict sun-protection regimen when I'm outdoors. Even a short amount of sun exposure leads to painful sunburns and/or freckles.

My bi-racial daughter doesn't burn, but that doesn't mean she is free from the risk of skin damage. Skin cancer risk and future wrinkles are on the line for her, just like the rest of us. When we're passing out sunscreen at the pool or theme park, we make sure everyone in the family is covered, and not just those of us who burn easily.

Caucasian hair

Some of you reading this book might have the opposite situation. Perhaps you are African American, bi-racial, or naturally curly and you're having to figure out how to deal with straight or wavy Caucasian hair.

My youngest daughter is Caucasian with pale skin and long, slightly-wavy red hair. Her hair is very thin and very fine. Making her hair look more healthy and full requires styling products (like mousse) and a curling iron. She has just enough natural wave in her hair to allow it to accept curls and if I've used styling products, the curls generally will last most of the day. She's very much of a girly girl and spends a lot of time trying out her own hairstyles, usually involving some sort of flower or bow (or more than one, if she can get away with it).

Here is her typical hair regimen:

- ❑ Wash with shampoo daily – some people shampoo every other day or follow a "no poo" method. I find that my child is too active to skip shampooing every day or her hair tends to have a slightly funky smell. Perhaps as she

gets older and isn't playing outside as much, we may reduce this to every other day.
- ❏ Conditioner daily. I use something different for her than her curly sister, just so they can feel like individuals, but they could easily use the same conditioner.
- ❏ Spritz with a de-tangler in the morning before she brushes her hair.
- ❏ Kids' mousse and a curling iron for special occasions, like picture day or Sunday morning church.

Hair is a big deal in our house because we have girls. It is less of a big deal with boys, although boys with natural curls need some extra effort and products, too. If you are unfamiliar in dealing with your child's particular hair, invest in a good hair stylist who can give you advice.

Chapter 11
Broken records

When I was a child I wanted to grow up and become a detective. My brother and I even formed our own detective agency. All the crimes we solved were imaginary and involved low-level mysteries like "Who stole the candy?" I outgrew that dream (and *several* others) before settling on a real career in adulthood.

I got to re-live my childhood dream upon bringing the girls home. One of the unexpected "joys" of adopting an older child from the foster system is the detective work you have to do to uncover their complete records.

Children's Division records

When my husband and I went through the adoption licensing classes, our instructors told us repeatedly to look at the Children's Division records before adoption was finalized. Missouri is a closed adoption state, meaning that once the adoption is finalized, the record is permanently sealed and can only be opened with a judge's order – which is rarely ever granted.

We were told not to make photocopies, but that we could otherwise copy down as many details as we wanted. Our caseworker encouraged us to note as many biological family names, dates and details as possible, along with any medical records and anything else that could possibly be useful later in the child's life.

My husband and I made a trip to the county where our girls entered foster care and the caseworker let us spend as long as we wanted with the records, which were contained in three very large three-ring binders. Many of the documents reflected the bureaucracy of the foster care system, which required a form to document every tiny thing. I skipped past a lot of the documents for this reason.

However, many documents listed various biological family members, where they lived, and noteworthy information about each. There was a fairly detailed medical history for each biological parent involved in the case and a somewhat detailed medical history for each of the children. Details of the caseworker visits were less helpful, although these notes filled in some blanks of why transitions were made from one foster placement to another. I gained very little information from court documents other than to be frustrated by how many times a judge allowed the case to linger without any progress.

I filled a notebook with as many details as I thought I would ever need, either for myself or for the girls if they ever want to know more about that period of their life. That notebook has been tucked away for safekeeping and I'm sure will be used quite a bit as they grow older.

Educational records

My girls moved once while in their biological parents home and shortly thereafter moved when they entered their first foster placement and again four months later for their second placement. A year later they were on to their third placement before meeting us a year later and starting at their current school. Tracking down the complete record of their grades, test scores, attendance, immunizations, and all the other educational records has been interesting to say the least.

In this process I have discovered that some records officers (usually the school secretary) are *very* helpful and kind, but that is definitely not true for them all. In one district – interestingly, the one the girls attended the longest – it took four different requests, a couple of phone calls and several emails to receive a response. When they finally did respond, what I was told didn't completely line up with what the rest of the records reflected. Critical documents were lost or unavailable, according to the secretary. It seemed that the school was intentionally trying to thwart my attempts to understand what happened during the gaps in the documentation they were willing to provide.

It has been a frustrating process and it has been tough to keep my Mad Momma Bear instincts at bay. In the end it appears that my oldest daughter got lost in the system and decisions were made that left her chances of success very vulnerable if she had remained in that school district.

Getting a complete educational record for my children allowed me to advocate for them in our local school district. While it was important to me that they have a complete record, it was even more important for the school to understand what was previously done and what needed to happen next. I highly recommend that other foster-adopt parents do the leg-work to track down as complete a record as you can.

Here are the things most helpful to obtain:

- ❏ Grade cards from all schools for every available quarter/semester
- ❏ Title I records of services received (this isn't always available, but ask anyway)
- ❏ Special education records including evaluations, if applicable
- ❏ 504 Plans, if applicable
- ❏ Behavioral records (Were they ever suspended? Did they receive services from a Special Education teacher specifically for behavior?)
- ❏ Attendance records
- ❏ Immunization records

Medical records and immunizations, too

One of the hardest things to get as a foster-adopt parent is a full medical record. If the parents were a hot mess, you can bet they didn't keep an organized record of their child's medical care (assuming care was even provided). Parents living in abject poverty are unlikely to have health insurance, which means they don't have a regular pediatrician or pediatric dentist. Often, health services are provided by the emergency room at the local hospital because the ER can't turn away patients who can't pay. Immunizations for school are often provided by the local health department and it is up to the parent to maintain the records.

Additionally, families living in poverty are often considered transient, meaning they don't stay in one place very long. A family might move into an apartment, live for six months until the landlord evicts them for failure to pay rent, and then move to another apartment or a trailer home in the next town over. These moves aren't made with well-organized, neatly-labeled boxes and a U-Haul truck. Desperate parents may grab the most important stuff that will fit in the trunk of the car as they hurry to avoid local law enforcement. They leave the rest of their belongings behind.

What this all means for the foster-adopt parent is that health records are nearly impossible to piece together. Even a complete immunization record is rarely available. Schools are a great source to get shot records, but it may not reflect accurately all the immunizations a child has had in their lifetime.

We were lucky. Our girls had a caseworker whose relationship with their biological mother was fairly positive. The medical record she included in their case file was informative and included a minor surgery one girl had as a toddler and stitches the other girl had at age five. The record also included everything biological mom could remember of her own health record and anything she could remember about the health of the girls' fathers. We have a more thorough record than most foster families receive.

Even with this relative wealth of information, there are a lot of blanks we can't fill in. There are many questions to which we will never know the answers. Luckily, I have contact information for some of the biological relatives. If something dramatic were to happen with the health of either girl, we have a way to contact the biological relatives, if we needed to. This will also allow the girls to get more details to fill in the blanks of their own health history someday.

When I signed up to become an adoptive parent, I didn't realize I was also signing up to be a detective. I certainly haven't solved all the mysteries and I'm not as cool as Remington Steele or Veronica Mars, but filling in as many blanks as possible has already been worth the effort.

Chapter 12
Getting schooled

A huge part of parenting any child is navigating the education system. Whether you choose a public, private, or parochial school or choose to homeschool your kids, there's a good chance you'll have your hands on your child's learning process.

For me, I have a background in education. Plus, I am passionate about people discovering who they are meant to be and achieving it. When thinking about education for my own children, I want to make sure the doors are all open for them to pursue who they are meant to be in their adult career. That means I'm actively involved in their learning and I am well acquainted with their academic strengths and weaknesses.

One Thousand Questions

Since bringing our girls home, we have "enjoyed" *many* questions from Little Sister. It is a bit like living with a toddler who constantly asks questions to understand the world.

We initially thought the questions were driven by a "poverty of experience" in her early childhood. Questions are most prominent when we watch movies. Little Sister asks a constant stream of questions during movie nights at our house. She can't wrap her brain around the relationships between characters or make inferences about what is happening in the plot. From one moment to the next she forgets who a character is or why they behave the way they do. She is always interested to know which characters "like each other" and often makes hilarious guesses about the romantic interests of characters. For example, we were watching a movie where the young man's mother was featured prominently in the storyline. We had discussed who this character was. Even so, during one scene between the mother and son, my daughter innocently asked, "Do they *like* each other?"

Here's a typical movie conversation:

During "Harry Potter: Prisoner of Azkaban" [**Note:** *this is at least the third time we have watched this movie together*]:

> **Little:** Who is Harry looking for?
> **Me:** Peter Petticrew...but Harry doesn't know he's disguised as Ron's rat so Harry doesn't notice him in the dark hallway.
> **Little:** [*later in the movie*] Why did the mouse bite Ron?!
> **Husband:** Because the rat is Peter Petticrew who is disguised. He's trying to get away from Ron.
> **Me:** Peter is a bad guy, remember?
> **Little:** [*later in the movie*] Why are they trying to get Ron's mouse?!
> **Husband:** Remember that isn't just a mouse, it's Peter Petticrew...who is a bad guy.
> **Little:** [*after the rat turns into the human form of Peter Petticrew*] What happened to the rat?! Who is *that* guy?!
> **Me:** Remember the several times we have talked about Peter Petticrew and how he pretended to be Ron's rat?
> **Little:** Huh?

Houston we (might) have a problem

As time has worn on in parenting Little Sister, we have discovered that the questions might be a signal or a symptom of something larger. Perhaps she isn't just trying to understand the world with her million questions. We started to wonder about a disability in language. We had always just informally "diagnosed" her as being a ditzy kid. After a while, it became increasingly troubling that she couldn't make inferences or fully comprehend what people were saying to one another like other children her age could do. It made her thousand-silly-questions less hilarious and more disconcerting. That started our quest to have her evaluated for a possible disability.

One of the great things about living in the United States of America is that we, the taxpayers, are promised a Free Appropriate Public Education (FAPE) for our children. That means our government is required to provide an education for all children, including those with a disability, at no cost to the parents (other than taxes, of course, and all those infuriating school fundraisers).

The "appropriate" portion of that description is a little more confusing to most people. Appropriate for one child may not be appropriate for another. What is appropriate for an ideal-learner with a 130 IQ might not be the same as what will work for a non-verbal child with a 65 IQ who is confined to a wheelchair.

To deal with the "appropriate" provision, the government has a provision called Individuals with Disabilities Education Act (IDEA), which provides federal funding to schools to educate children diagnosed with a federally-recognized disability. This legislation is designed to meet FAPE requirements that are tailored to the individual needs of students with a disability.

This is done by first being referred for evaluation. Often this referral is made by the classroom teacher who has tried a variety of possible solutions to a child's educational weaknesses without success. There is often a referral process that involves other professionals at the school, including classroom teacher, school counselor, special education teachers, a school psychologist, and a process coordinator (someone who coordinates the administrative processes related to special education). Parents are included in the referral process as soon as the classroom teacher suspects there is a problem.

In our case, Little Sister's social anxiety kept her from being noticed in the classroom. She flew under the radar in her class of 25 students because she was quiet and worked hard at blending in. Little Sister was keeping her head above water largely by watching what the people around her did and copying their actions. She wasn't exactly cheating in the intentional sense, but she definitely wasn't doing 100% of the work correctly all by herself. Truth be told, I think the other kids felt sorry for her and fed her answers so she wouldn't be embarrassed.

Because of her stealthy ways, her classroom teacher didn't understand what we were talking about when we brought up the learning struggles we saw at home. Luckily, Little Sister had been going with a small group of students to work with a reading specialist for part of the school day, and that special teacher saw all the same struggles we were seeing at home.

With the reading specialist's validation in hand, we made our own referral for an evaluation. This is something parents have the right to do if they are concerned about their child's learning.

Once the referral has made it to the team, they determine which kinds of assessments might be needed to determine what is happening with a child to keep them from learning as they should. There will almost always be a hearing and vision screening by the school nurse, an IQ test (either verbal or non-verbal), and an achievement test. These are the basics that are typically "ordered" first in a special education evaluation.

Depending on the concerns, other tests might be ordered to determine things like reading fluency, expressive language, auditory memory, and the like.

In a typical evaluation, the special education staff is looking to see how large the gap is between what the child ought to be able to do (their IQ) and what they actually can do (such as their score on the achievement test). If the gap is large enough, the child will qualify for services and accommodations based on that specific gap or disability. If the gap is not large enough, the team might try to find other options to improve the weakness, but it will be outside of the requirements detailed in IDEA.

Little Sister's gap wasn't large enough in any area, although the evaluation team could see there were weaknesses that needed to be addressed. The decision was made to place her in a classroom where there was a regular classroom teacher and a full-time special education support teacher to provide extra attention and resources to struggling students. Little Sister would be treated like the other traditional students in that class unless she was struggling with a concept or subject and then she would receive some learning support from the "extra" teacher who was there to help the special education students in that classroom. It ended up being a very successful year and the extra resources allowed her to thrive in some of her weak areas. It wasn't a complete solution, but it was better than nothing.

Since Little Sister didn't qualify for an Individualized Education Plan under IDEA, we could have pursued a different option. Because she has a diagnosis of A.D.H.D., we could have pursued a 504 Plan. The Rehabilitation Act of 1973 has protections for individuals with disabilities or long-term illnesses; this is meant to protect them from discrimination. Section 504 of this federal statute requires that the needs of an individual be met as well as those of a non-disabled individual. Schools don't all apply this statute as evenly as they do the provisions in IDEA. Some school districts are very open to 504 accommodations for students, other districts scoff when the idea is presented by parents.

A 504 Plan may be a good option to ask about if your child does not qualify for an individualized education plan, but would benefit from accommodations to help them be successful in school. This might include a child with Tourette's Syndrome, dyslexia, A.D.D./A.D.H.D., a long-term illness, or other conditions that might interfere with major life activities, such as school performance.

For example, a student who has Type I diabetes might require the school to accommodate the testing, insulin injection, and snack requirements so that the child's blood sugar levels can be maintained at a healthy level. A 504 Plan in this case would be written to make sure all school adults are aware of the child's needs and which accommodations are needed to ensure school success.

In the case of a child with A.D.D. or A.D.H.D. who struggles to focus during paper and pencil tasks, a 504 Plan could be written to include certain accommodations like testing under un-timed circumstances or testing in an alternate (read "quiet") location. Another accommodation may be using a computer to type written work (like essays) rather than using a pencil and paper, since this type of task can be challenging for children with A.D.H.D.

Dear Future Teacher

Each year I write a letter to my children's teachers to introduce them and make sure the teacher knows which quirks to expect. This task was most important the first couple of years with the girls when they had more issues they were working to overcome. Here's a sample letter:

"Dear [*Little Sister's Teacher*],

I hope you're enjoying your week of back-to-school teacher meetings and getting your classroom ready for the year.

I am writing to introduce you to my daughter, [*Little Sister*]. We adopted her in November of 2013 after she had bounced around foster care for almost two years. She is a very quiet, sweet girl, but there are some things I would like to share with you that might not be obvious about my girl. She has done great in the adoption transition, but is sometimes sad as she thinks about her biological family members. Let me know if this ever interferes with her ability to succeed at school.

She is an easy girl to get lost in a crowd. She has a history of social anxiety and takes a very long time to warm up to new people. She hates being embarrassed and will do almost anything to avoid that. This means she isn't one to volunteer for tasks where people will look at her and will take a long time to become comfortable being called on to give answers in front of the whole class.

She also has A.D.H.D., which we have had diagnosed by a psychologist. You probably won't notice a lot of her hyperactivity because her social anxiety keeps that in check. She works really hard not to draw attention to herself in public, so it would be easy to miss her A.D.H.D. symptoms. However, she might be looking at you like everyone else in the class, but she is very likely thinking about other things inside her mind. [*Little Sister*] is very easily distracted. Her mental process is also very disorganized, especially where language tasks are concerned. She has a hard time making inferences and answering questions that require her to think critically.

It is difficult for [*Little Sister*] to follow multi-step directions, especially if they are only given verbally. She also tends to be a perfectionist, which causes her to sometimes work at a slow pace and then miss what she was supposed to be doing when everyone else moved on. Ideally, directions would be written down for her to follow as she works at her own pace. This also affects her ability to remember what she is supposed to do for homework. She wants to comply with adult requests, but her working memory keeps her from remembering what she is supposed to do long enough to accomplish the task the way adults asked her to do it. She ends up very frustrated at herself for her inability to do what will make the adults in her life happy.

[*Little Sister*] is a kind-hearted, fun-loving child once she gets to know you and you are going to love having her in your class. I can't wait to see what happens this year with you as her teacher.

Blessings,
"Mom"

Chapter 13
Poking the momma bear

One thing you'll find as an adoptive parent is how fiercely it makes you defend your children. Most parents stand behind their kids and protect them from harm, but something special happens in adoption that puts those protective instincts on steroids.

My kids have already been dealt a lousy hand as far as life experiences go, and I'll be darned if I'm going to stand by and let it happen again. Part of that defense-of-my-children instinct is always ready to spring into parental action if someone seems to be treating my children wrongly.

I'm appreciating how different adoption is than giving birth. There are experiences we have that "real" parents don't have. Bonding with adopted kids is different. Dissecting their behaviors to see which are normal and which need to be discussed in therapy is different. People sometimes react differently to adoptive families than they do biological families.

Even the way we bring our new "babies" home is treated differently sometimes. When a new mom and dad are nearing delivery date of their new oven-bun, there are showers and meal trains. That doesn't always happen in the foster-adopt process. This can make the adoptive parents feel alone; like their big event is important to no one but themselves. There's a loneliness about adoption because so much of the experience is either misunderstood by others or we just aren't allowed to share the details due to confidentiality.

All these things have a cumulative effect on our parental brains and it sometimes makes us quick to jump into defense mode. A few items have pushed my buttons over the years and Mad Momma Bear has reared her head.

"Oh....all kids do that."
Sometimes I wonder about my children. Since my husband

and I didn't have biological children, we don't have experience parenting "normal" kids. But, I've worked with kids for years as a teacher and social worker. I have also worked in a group home with 7-12 year old psychiatric patients. I've got an idea of what normal and abnormal looks like with kids from all those years of experience.

What I've noticed, however, is that when I say something about a behavior challenge we are having, I am often met with a pat on the head from my biological-parent friends. "Oh....all kids do that."

What they don't realize, though, is that my children's behavior issue is often more intense, more frequent, more lengthy in duration, and sometimes has a more unusual trigger than it would be in a normal child. During the first year, my youngest child had tantrums whenever she heard the word "no". Her response was far beyond what you would expect given the thing she was frustrated about. The tantrums were frequent and lasted a long time. They were also intense, with loud, shrill screaming and hiding under the bed or furniture in her room long after the incident should have ended.

When people told us "Oh...all kids do that", they were most likely trying to offer parental solidarity over a shared experience they too have had with tantrums. It's like parents getting together and lamenting the difficulty of potty training or getting your child to do their homework. But, the unintended effect of the words "Oh...all kids do that" is that it degrades the Black Hole of parenting that we are sometimes trapped in with a particularly troubling behavior. "Oh...all kids do that" isn't actually as helpful or comforting as anyone thinks, especially when you've been struggling day in and day out with that behavior and even your therapist isn't sure how to help.

"She's so sweet at [literally any place other than home]...are you sure you aren't just too sensitive about her behavior."

Most children, whether adopted or biological, behave differently at school or church or grandma's house than they do at home. Your home is their safe place, the one place in the world where they are most comfortable being their true self.

Just think of yourself: don't you come home from work, wash off your make-up, change into sweatpants, and turn into a different person than everyone else in the world gets to see? And aren't you more likely to snap meanly to your spouse than you are to your co-worker, fellow churchgoer, or yoga instructor? In fact, you know you've reached a new and wonderful stage in a relationship when you let your guard down enough to be unpleasant without worry (Hint: think about the first time you farted in front of your significant other and he/she loved you anyway).

It's no different for children. They spend a lot of time following the rules at school to avoid being embarrassed in front of the other kids or getting a bad reputation. Like us, they don't want neighbors or people from church or their coach or Grandpa to see them in a negative light. They put on their best self in those settings. But at home, their parents and siblings get to witness their true selves. We know the person they are when they are tired and cranky or when they are frustrated. Our children show us their truest personality at home.

And that's a good thing because it means we are safe and we will love them despite their unpleasantness.

"Are they 'real'?"

One day at school I was asked by one of my fourth graders about an upcoming event.

> **Student:** Are you going to come see us perform?
> **Me:** No. I'm afraid I can't.
> **Student:** [*sarcastically*] Oh, I suppose you have to take care of your [*finger quotes*] "daughters", right?
> **Me:** I'm not sure why you're using finger quotes, since they are real girls and they really are my children. I can show you a picture of them.
> **Student:** Right. I know they're [*finger quotes*] "real"...but

they're adopted, right?
Me: Yes, they're adopted, but they are still really my daughters. That statement doesn't need finger quotes.
Student: But they're your [*finger quotes*] "daughters", not your [*finger quotes*] "real" daughters.

This little interaction got me to thinking about how people often perceive adopted children versus "real" children. When people use the word "real" in relation to children, what they mean is actually "biological". It takes a little education to help people understand how to talk about adoption.

Most people approve of adoption. Even most cold-hearted folks want children to have a family instead of wandering the streets.

However, I have been surprised by how many people ask awkward adoption questions. I once saw a great video put together by a pastor, named Jesse Butterworth, which compared questions about adoption to questions about a boob job. If you wouldn't ask "Are they real?" to a woman in regards to her breasts, then you shouldn't ask the question about her children.

Are they both "yours"?

When people ask this particular question, they're trying to make sense of the mismatched image they see in our family. I think most people ask this particular question because the girls don't look anything alike, so most people assume they were adopted separately or that one is biological and the other adopted. Most people who meet my two daughters think that the younger one looks like me. We both have fair skin and reddish hair. And our similar looks are one of the things that swayed the adoption staffing in our favor. However, that is a hard question for us to hear at our house. While my youngest child always beams with pride at that question, my older daughter wilts when she hears it. It is no fun to be left out and that question always makes her feel like she is less than her sister just because of her looks.

If you see a family that looks like a mixed bag and it is clear that adoption must have been involved, stay away from personal questions about who are biologically-related and who are not. Try not to gush over how much one child looks like a parent if it will exclude another child who is standing in earshot. There is so much pain that can be triggered by treating children differently, especially based purely on looks.

Didn't you ever want children of our own?

I personally loathe this question, mostly because it has been asked with such frequency. This is a question that should only be asked by someone well within the circle of influence of the person being questioned. This might be a legitimate question for your very best friend who has adopted and you've never talked about the motivation behind it. Only broach this subject if you are doing so in love and out of interest for your friend's feelings and experiences.

In my case, it is a question without emotion or pain behind it. Honestly, I have never had a desire to give birth to children. In my opinion, giving birth doesn't make you a mom, parenting does. These girls are my own children, even if I didn't give birth to them. It doesn't make me sad in the least to look back on my decision to adopt because I made it proudly at age twelve.

However, that's not the journey every adoptive parent has taken. I know people who arrived at the decision to adopt after first grieving the dream to have biological children. For folks in that category, this question is painful. Asking if they ever wanted "children of [their] own" raises uncomfortable memories about the fertility treatments they endured and the devastation they felt knowing the journey to starting a family wasn't going to happen the way they had always imagined. While they may be completely sold on adoption now that they've done it, that may not have been the case when they started the adoption journey.

Sometimes life hands you lemons...sometimes it hands you idiots on the Internet

Sometimes it isn't a question that will poke the Mad Momma Bear. Occasionally, the issues that affect your child will come up as an Internet discussion or debate and will make you want to scream from the rooftop to correct the world's misconceptions.

Recently, a friend of mine went to Facebook to lament that the emergency room required her to show proof that she was the parent of her son, who was adopted from Haiti. He has the same last name she has. She had a valid, current copy of his health insurance and her own driver's license to prove they have matching last names. The only thing she didn't have was the same color skin as her son, which triggered the hospital intake person to require proof of guardianship.

My friend and I share a common lament. My husband, my youngest daughter and I have white skin, my oldest daughter has brown skin. When we go places, my daughter's brown skin makes her stand out from the rest of us...and she is keenly aware of that fact. She doesn't need the intake person at urgent care to point that out by asking only for guardianship papers proving she is part of our family, but never asking the same thing for her white sister.

While having this conversation on Facebook, my friend's acquaintance started commenting about how it isn't that big of a deal to show proof-of-guardianship for African-American children and that it really is to "protect" all kids. "You just aren't seeing the bigger picture" he asserted. "The world isn't being racist to you" he claimed. "Your anger over this is clouding your judgment" he suggested. "You are overreacting by acting miserable just because you have to show your guardianship papers sometimes."

I'm still unclear why he thought I was "overreacting" or "miserable" when all I said was that it would be nice if the same policy on proof-of-guardianship applied equally to all minors and not just the brown-skinned ones. Who knows what lines he was reading between to see some sort of unspoken inner turmoil or out-of-control rage that even I didn't know I was experiencing. Social media is often good for misunderstandings.

No matter what I tried saying to this internet "enthusiast", I couldn't get him to see that I don't expect to have ER or urgent care intake workers look at my daughter and assume she came out of my vagina. However, they shouldn't look at my white daughter to make that assumption either (since she also didn't come out of my vagina).

If health care administrators or others are worried about guardianship, shouldn't they worry about that for all children? I could just as easily attempt to scam the system with a white, non-related child as I could with a black, Latino, or Asian one. Wouldn't it be simpler just to extend the policy so that all adults presenting a child for treatment at urgent care or the ER have proof-of-guardianship (or other rights to pursue medical care)?

The idiot on the Internet kept chipping away at my patience that day. However, as he raised my ire, he also raised my concern about the pervasive nature of the race issues we face. Is it really so rare for white parents to have adopted children of a different race that people literally don't know what to do with families like mine? And what can I do to improve the situation for other families?

My main take away from my Internet interaction with Mr. Troll McClueless was that when life hands you idiots, make sure you have taken your blood pressure pills and prayed to Jesus for an extra measure of kindness to love the idiot despite his (or her) stupidity.

Unfortunately, this will not be my last frustration over people making false assumptions or idiots making ridiculous comments on the Internet. Sometimes adoption means resigning yourself to the misinformation of others and their verbal-vomit.

Chapter 14
FAQ's

Over the years I have fielded a lot of questions from people interested in adoption. My answers relate to the way Missouri does things, but the other states aren't dramatically different in most cases. The Internet is your friend in researching what is true for your state; or take your question to the local agency that handles foster care in your area. Adoption caseworkers are usually more than happy to answer questions specific to your state.

Here are a few of the most common questions I have been asked:

Is it expensive to adopt through the foster care system?
It is not expensive at all to adopt through the foster care system. In fact, we were only out the cost of gas and any food we ate if we traveled to and from different adoption interviews (called "staffings") or meetings. Even those costs could be turned in for reimbursement if we wanted to pursue that option. The adoption court costs, our lodging and travel costs for the adoption court date, the lawyer's fees, and everything else were covered by the State of Missouri. We didn't even see bills for most items and if we did, we turned them over to our adoption caseworker and that was the last we saw of it.

Are there any benefits that help offset costs after you adopt?
Most states offer some sort of financial assistance or services for children adopted through foster care. There is an idea that the state doesn't want to be in the business of raising orphans and the outcomes are best for kids in permanent, loving homes. Offering financial assistance to help with the costs of caring for children is one way to create incentives for adoption by removing barriers.

- ✓ ***Monthly stipends*** – In the State of Missouri, foster parents receive a monthly payment as "professional parents". It isn't what you could make at a job, so it isn't any sort of payment that could replace a regular income. This amount is exclusive to foster parents and ends once the adoption is finalized. There is also a monthly "maintenance" payment for each child in foster or foster-adopt care to offset the costs of raising them, like food, clothing, school supplies, and extra-curricular opportunities. The monthly maintenance payment continues after adoption. Again, this amount of money isn't enough to be a living wage for the foster or adoptive parent. The money does come in handy because kids are expensive. If your kids are like mine you'll wonder where all the food went and why your water bill is suddenly doubled.

- ✓ ***Medical Care*** – One big cost for many families is heath insurance. The State of Missouri allows children to stay on MO HealthNet insurance (i.e., Medicaid) through age 18. This covers medical care (annual visits, urgent care, emergency room visits, specialists, surgeries, etc.), prescriptions, dental, and vision. We have never been denied any services and we never see a bill.

- ✓ ***Daycare*** – Another big expense for many working parents is childcare. The State of Missouri recognizes this and covers childcare expenses at certain approved daycares for children age zero to twelve. Once my child turned thirteen it was assumed she could stay at home alone. If we had concerns about her developmental ability to stay home safely (as might be the case for a child with a developmental or physical disability, for example), our caseworker would have helped us explore our options. The childcare options we had available to us were wonderful, safe, and clean. We always felt that we had positive options for childcare with our foster-adopt kids.

- ✓ ***Counseling*** – I highly recommend counseling for your child(ren) if you are going through the foster-adoption process. Even if everything is smooth sailing and they are the most well-adjusted kids ever born, the adoption process is a big change and involves a lot of loss for the child. They've lost biological family members and their identity. Leaving their biological home involves leaving behind cherished belongings, pets, neighbors, and comfortable experiences. Foster care and adoption also sometimes brings changes in schools, which brings loss of friendships, beloved teachers, and others the child may have trusted. Counseling is critical as kids navigate these hard feelings and children need a safe, trusted adult they can talk to without worry over how it might affect their adoptive parents' feelings. Our adoption caseworker helped us find an appropriate counselor for our children and the cost has been completely covered by their MO HealthNet insurance. I highly recommend that all adoptive parents seek this same benefit, even if they only use it temporarily.

- ✓ ***Support from a Caseworker*** – One of the benefits of adopting through the foster care system, at least in Missouri, is that you remain under the caseload of a person whose job it is to make adoptions successful. We love our adoption caseworker and she has been helpful so many times throughout this process, even after the adoption was finalized. We even sometimes pick up her favorite lunch and show up at her office just so we can see her. One of our fellow adoptive parents has had to use his family's adoption worker to access mental health services as one child experienced crisis after crisis in her struggle with mental illness. The caseworker helped them make arrangements for a short-term stay in a behavioral health hospital and in finding a long-term solution in a group home until the child was able to emerge on the other side with a treatment plan to return home safely. Whether it is questions about a particular behavior, advice about how to answer tricky adoption questions, help in accessing needed services, or getting together for a game night; the ongoing support from an adoption caseworker is one of our favorite benefits.

- ✓ **Tax Relief –** Varying amounts of tax relief might be available depending on your state. Be sure to ask your tax accountant about possible tax benefits for adopting through foster care.

What is the benefit of foster adoption over private or international adoption?

Aside from the numerous areas of financial and parental support you receive if you adopt from the foster care system, there are other benefits that are just as important. One benefit is getting to know the child before the adoption is final. Just like the placement is considered legal risk and could, in theory, be over-turned if the birth parents' rights don't end up being terminated; the placement does allow for a trial period with the child before the adoption date. While certainly not an ideal situation, if a child enters your family and just isn't a fit at all or has behaviors that your family just can't handle (like harming pets or displaying sexual behavior toward other children in the home), then a family can change their mind. Caseworkers have the option of treating it like any other foster placement during that six-month "waiting period".

The foster care system also gives families quite a bit of information about the child before he or she is placed in a family. Generally, a child or their family has a history in the system that goes back months, except in the case of an infant who is removed at birth due to drug exposure. The experience caseworkers and previous foster parents have with a child is well-documented for potential adoptive parents. This isn't usually the case with international adoptions. In the United States, caseworkers aren't interested in risking failed adoptions, so they make certain that parents know what they are getting into with a particular child. International adoptions sometimes rely on sources who are being paid to see children adopted out, which makes "orphans" a commodity in some countries. This means some foreign adoption workers aren't as interested in giving out information that could turn off potential "buyers" of their "product".

The Termination of Parental Rights (TPR) is also more secure when completed through the foster-adoption process. So many steps have been taken over months or years of work with parents that judges are almost never willing to overturn a TPR once it is granted. The same process that seems to take forever is partly meant to protect the new adoptive placement from failing, since this isn't in the best interest of the child.

Does the state interfere with your rights as parents?

While the girls were still considered foster children, there were several restrictions placed on us. We couldn't take them out of state for more than a day trip without permission from the judge. We couldn't make any drastic changes to their hair other than to maintain their normal hairstyle through a trim.

The state also restricts what you share about your child while they are in the foster system. It's called "confidentiality" and you are bound by certain rules to protect your child's identity as someone in foster care. That means you cannot refer to them by name or post pictures of them on social media. For those of us who are addicted to Facebook or Instagram (or whatever is popular with the "cool kids" these days), this restriction will be the most challenging to uphold. We did post about the girls, but they were referred to only as "Big" and "Little" online (a practice we have continued post-adoption). We posted a few pictures, but we either covered their face with a smile emoji or we took the picture so that their faces were not shown. This doesn't limit how many pictures you can take or print of your child, it just means you can't make those photos public until adoption is finalized.

There were meetings we were required to participate in, such as monthly case team reviews, and we had monthly visits with caseworkers in our home. There are other requirements for foster parents if the children still have contact with biological family members. There may be weekly or bi-weekly visits that a foster parent might have to transport the child(ren) to if that is the case.

When some people ask this question they are using the word "interfere" in relation to church attendance or religious practices. Our girls had gone to church with two out of the three foster families they lived with before coming to us. They enjoyed church and wanted to continue going after they joined our family. I would say most kids are open to attending services with a foster or adoptive family.

However, the older the child is, the more opinion they may have on this subject. As with any child, whether adopted or biological, forcing them to attend church as a teenager could easily backfire and turn them off to church indefinitely.

While I would caution against forcing any child to attend church if they don't want to go, that choice was up to us as parents. The state didn't put any restrictions on our choice to encourage church attendance with any of the children we fostered. The fear of "separation of church and state" in relation to parenting a foster or adopted child is an unfounded fear.

My husband and I have recently made the decision to homeschool our daughters. The state would have restricted this decision while the girls were in foster care because they needed proof that the child was receiving an adequate education, proof of attendance, etc. However, our caseworker has been very supportive of our decision to educate the girls at home now that the adoption is final. We have not faced interference from the state on this decision.

I realize it's December, but can I have a kid by Christmas?

Obviously, a big question has to do with how long it will take to get through the whole process. Sometimes people see photos of kids online for organizations like The Heart Gallery and fall in love with the idea of that specific child. Or maybe they are just too excited to wait through all the parts of the process. Our adoption caseworker, who we lovingly refer to "Curly-haired Sarah", actually had someone ask her in December if it was possible to adopt a child by Christmas (FYI – It's not possible).

Here are a few considerations in your timeline:
- ❑ Completing and submitting the initial application will take as long as you like for it to take. If you're a procrastinator, you probably won't even make it to the end of this sentence before putting down this book and forgetting to finish reading the rest of the steps. If you're a Type A perfectionist, you've probably already completed your form and submitted it yesterday because you built your own time machine to allow you to accomplish things before the instructions were ever given. We submitted our paperwork in mid-January of 2012.
- ❑ Getting onto the roster for an upcoming foster-adoption class can be immediate or take six months, depending on the availability of the class. In our county there are multiple sessions of the S.T.A.R.S. classes for foster-parent licensing each year. The classes are 27 hours total and can be offered in a variety of ways, from multiple evenings each week to long Saturday sessions. We got into the S.T.A.R.S. session that started in February and ended in mid-April of 2012.
- ❑ The Spaulding classes are also offered several times each year, usually within a few weeks of the final S.T.A.R.S. session that preceded it. Again, the timing of that depends on when it is scheduled and how long the waiting list for the class is. The Spaulding classes are twelve hours total. Our Spaulding class started in early-June and we were officially licensed by early July of 2012.
- ❑ The home study process and background checks happen concurrently with the licensing classes, so you should finish the whole process by the end of the final course.

- ❏ The length of time it takes to matched with a kid depends on whether you plan to be a foster parent who eventually adopts or if you make the decision to be "adopt only". In the case of fostering, you could take a child home on the final night of your licensing classes (as was the case for someone in our class). For us, we were matched with the first sibling group about a month after our licensing process was complete, late-August of 2012.
- ❏ The State of Missouri requires a child to be living with their prospective adoptive parents for a minimum of six months. Had we been chosen for those first siblings and everything had gone 100% without a hitch, then our adoption date would have happened in late-February of 2013.
- ❏ In this hypothetical timeline, the process from initial application to adoption court date could have happened in one full-year. I would not count on it happening that smoothly. In our case, it took about 22 months to complete the entire application-to-adoption cycle.
- ❏ Nothing goes as smoothly as planned. I once heard someone say "Men plan, God laughs" and this saying is definitely true of the adoption process.

Those classes sound <u>super</u> boring and I just want to adopt right away. Can't I just do that?

Our adoption caseworker often gets questions about accelerating the adoption process by skipping over the (maybe a little boring) S.T.A.R.S. classes. People wonder why they need to become foster-licensed if they only want to adopt. Part of the explanation involves the goals of the entire system: reunification with biological parents as the first priority. If people could skip over the foster parenting step, the idea that these are someone else's children might get lost in the rush. It is critically important to understand this and to realize all the grief and loss that are tied to it.

The foster-licensing process is also important because you

will be a foster parent to these children during the six months (or more) they live in your home before adoption can be legally finalized. The government isn't in the business of creating orphans by terminating parental rights willy-nilly. There are many points along the way where the biological parents could turn the process around and successfully parent their children. The entire process is designed for that possibility to work out before the judge's gavel strikes that final time (or, as it was in our case, the gavel thing is purely theoretical).

For those months when you are waiting for an adoption court date, you are still legally considered to be a foster parent of children who are a legal risk. The biological parents could petition the court to consider new evidence that they have, in fact, met the requirements to be considered fit-to-parent. This is why foster licensing is important because you will be fostering the children, even as you hope and pray the day will come when they are legally yours.

Okay, I guess I can survive the boring classes at the beginning, but that's it, no more boring stuff....right?

Maintaining your foster-license involves some continuing hours of education for each year you are licensed. The state provides many educational opportunities throughout the year to meet this obligation. Most of the courses are very interesting and worthwhile.

What's in a home study? Are they going to check my zombie-apocalypse shelter?

My husband and I are a pretty organized and keep a clean home, even when there's not home-study "threat" hanging over our heads. The instructors of our S.T.A.R.S. course had already warned us what to expect in the home-study process, so we had already taken care of most of the items we knew they would check, like fire extinguishers, outlet covers, and smoke alarms. When the caseworker arrived to go over our house, there weren't very many items we had to correct.

A few people in our S.T.A.R.S. class weren't so lucky and had major red flags in their home. One thing that caseworkers don't seem to love is guns or other weapons in the home. Troubled kids plus guns is a tough equation. If you are a gun enthusiast, you need to ask up front what that will mean for your ability to foster and/or adopt children in your state.

Ooooh! It's like shopping online for the perfect kid, right?
According to our adoption caseworker, she is often asked about adopting a specific kind of kid. The question goes like this: "Can I just ask for a baby (or preschooler or elementary or teen)?" or "I have all girls. Can I just get a boy (or vice versa)?"

As fun as that sounds, adoption is not like ordering from Starbucks or shopping on Amazon. It isn't Burger King where you can "have it your way". While the caseworker will try to match you with a child that meets your criteria, you'll wait a long time if you have some highly-specific criteria in mind. Choosing to be "adopt only" and asking for a baby will have you waiting the longest, especially if you have a particular gender in mind. And if you're looking to bring home a newborn straight from the hospital, you'd better be prepared to do some drug detox on that little bundle of (screaming) joy.

We did have something in mind as far as an age range, but the range was broad and we knew there would be plenty of options for us even if we limited the search to those available for an adopt-only family. My husband and I were interested in children old enough to be in school, but young enough that we would still have time to enjoy watching them grow up. We also wanted a sibling group, partly because we know those are the hardest kids to find permanent placements for and we were up for the challenge. Plus, having kids who were already part of a family seemed to make sense for us. For that reason, we requested a sibling group of up to four children ages 5-14. We didn't have any limits on boys or girls.

Our openness and flexibility made us a good candidate to find a fit without waiting on a list for months or years.

Oh, brother...(or sister)

One question that was obvious for us was accepting siblings. Our girls are half-sisters who share the same biological mother. They have an older half-brother, and a younger brother who is a half-sibling to one of my daughters and a full-sibling to the other. The brothers weren't part of the adoption "package" for a variety of reasons too complicated to detail in this story.

The circumstances are different for each child. You really need to consider your willingness to accept more than one child if you plan to adopt from the foster care system. I'm not sure the statistics, but I'd say that there aren't many truly "only-children" in foster care.

One thing our caseworker asked us to consider was siblings born after our girls were adopted. If their biological mother had more children and those children came into state custody, would we be willing to take them into our home? We had to consider what a baby (or two or three) would mean for our lifestyle since we are older. That never became an issue for us, but I know several people who ended up adopting the younger sibling(s) of a child they previously adopted. One family ended up with four children when they only intended to adopt one. The biological mother just kept having babies, about one each year.

Speaking of birth parents...

I remember during that first S.T.A.R.S. class, the instructors opened the class up for questions at the end of the evening. The bulk of the questions were about birth parents. "Do we have to keep contact?" "Will you tell them our names and where we live?" "Are we going to be safe?"

The answer is pretty simple: It's up to you. If you feel that the biological parent in your case is unsafe – either because of your own comfort level or because of something you know about their "crimes" – you can elect to keep some information private (like where you live).

It would be difficult to keep your name out of it, though, since you may be responsible for transporting the child to and from visits. I'm not sure how you could maintain anonymity if you are seeing them once each week.

One foster parent we know doesn't ever give her home address to anyone other than the caseworker. She keeps a hard-and-fast rule for all children her family accepts that the biological family will never come to their home. We knew the biological parents of a set of kids we fostered briefly, so there was some openness with information in that case, but we haven't released even the name of our town to the biological family of our girls.

Someday, our girls will want contact with their birth parents when they are emotionally-mature enough to handle it. When the time comes, we will help them get in touch with their biological family members and I'm sure the girls will share with them some details of their lives. We will have to decide at that point what details we are willing to share, like our hometown or address.

We have contacted the biological parents in our case. During the process of finalizing adoption details, I found myself in possession of biological mom's email address and biological dad's mailing address in prison. I send them updated photos of the girls a few times a year along with a brief update (devoid of any details about where we live). The updates are always pretty vague, almost 100% focused on things that are happy or uplifting. I don't want them worried about the girls or to heap guilty feelings upon the loss they both feel, so I try to stay positive in the messages. Both biological parents have written to thank me for taking care of their children.

This was our choice for how to handle birth parents, but this is by no means an endorsement that our way is the best way. Each situation is unique and should be treated that way, preferably in consultation with your caseworker and the child's therapist.

What are my options for finding kids to adopt?

Finding kids isn't like finding a pair of great boots. You don't shop around to see which agency offers the best deal or the cutest tots. However, there are some options as far as foster-adoption goes. We went with our state agency, which in Missouri is called Children's Division. Missouri also contracts foster care and adoption with a few agencies, such as: Missouri Baptist Children's Home (MBCH), Lutheran Family and Children's Services (LFCS), and Catholic Charities, just to name a few.

Some folks prefer going through a religiously-affiliated organization because they feel there will be less governmental "interference" in how they are allowed to raise the children. Other people prefer it because they hold a negative stereotype of state-run foster care. Just comparing notes to friends who have gone through MBCH for adoption has led me to believe it is essentially the same process that we experienced, just with nicer chairs at the licensing classes.

I would like to caution against falling in love with the professional photos on websites like Heart Gallery featuring foster children waiting for adoption. The chance of ending up with one of the featured children on such websites is very slim. If you choose to adopt through the foster system, you cannot control the experience by choosing the child out of a lineup of children on a website. Most every other aspect of life is under our control to choose, but it just doesn't work that way in this system. You can miss out on some really amazing kids if you rule out too many choices based on unrealistic expectations. Remain as open as possible and try to trust your adoption caseworker to make a match for you and your family.

Where do babies come from?

Since I'm answering questions, I thought I'd answer a question that I'm sure has been asked since the beginning of mankind: "Where do babies come from?"

I worked for a bunch of years as a school counselor at a private, Christian school and since we didn't have a school nurse, it always fell to me to give the "hygiene talk" to our fifth grade girls. Needless to say, I've given the-birds-and-the-bees talk a bunch of times in my career. I'm pretty good at it, although it isn't a skill I've ever managed to successfully include in my resume. I can explain the inner workings of the lady parts like a champ and I don't blush at all when using words like "erection", "ejaculation", and "wet dreams".

When it came time to give "the talk" to my own budding tween, the result was far less comfortable. She didn't make eye contact with me and acted as though I was slowly and painfully murdering her with the words "uterus" and "menstruation".

I refused to be dissuaded, however. Over the years since that terribly-traumatizing talk, we have continued to bring up uncomfortable issues like periods, tampons, bras, and boobs to help my girls see these topics as normal and not the-most-embarrassing-thing-*ever*.

When we talk about lady parts, we use the real terms. The same goes with male body parts. It is my belief that children and teens, especially young girls, need to hear the correct words for their body parts and what they are meant for. It demystifies these words and reduces the likelihood they will seek answers from Google and wind up taking an accidental bunny trail into the addictive world of pornography.

Additionally, it is more difficult for people to take advantage of girls who have been educated about their bodies and the rights they have to decide who does and does not touch them privately. It is a topic we talk about often so there are no questions about how to handle it if someone touches them or asks them to text nude or near-nude pictures.

I know some people fear teaching their children the real terminology for fear that they will use the words at church or in the middle of Target, but those fears have (so far) been unfounded in our experience. We've never had a child say anything like: "Pastor Jim, my mom says men have penises. Is that why you always keep one hand in your pocket while you're preaching?"

In answer to the question "Where do babies come from?": Hopefully not my daughters until they are married.

How do adopted kids feel about adoption?

Every child is different in how they feel about adoption. Even my two children have vastly different approaches to it. One child has a very cut-and-dry approach to her past and present. She didn't have a good experience in her life before adoption, so she isn't interested in looking in the rearview mirror at the past. My other child had a much more positive experience and spends a lot more time thinking and dreaming about the past. Many of her memories are romanticized and, because she was so little at the time, there are lots of gaps in what she understood about her parents' negative choices as they were happening. Her positive memories of the past keep her more fixed on wanting the past to be part of her present and future life. Both of my girls' reactions to adoption are perfectly normal.

One thing they both have in common is that they are happy in their adopted life and are glad to have adoptive parents. In fact, both girls have mentioned that they may adopt their own children someday.

As happy as they are to be adopted, both girls have needed some coaching in how to talk about adoption when asked by outsiders. We have given them a few "canned" responses to questions, which has helped them feel comfortable and confident.

What do I tell my family about my adoption plans?

If you scan social media or peruse Pinterest very often, you're bound to come across about a million different ways to announce your birth or celebrate finding out the sex of your unborn child. But, alas, there aren't many ideas to be had for announcing plans to adopt.

In my case, my closest people all knew about my plans well before anything happened. But, as you might have guessed from reading this book so far, I'm not your typical case.

Honesty is the best policy when it comes to announcing plans to adopt. Start with your closest friends and family, the ones most likely to be affected by the news.

Unless you have just opened this book and started reading at this exact paragraph, you are already keenly aware of the challenges of adopting a child who has a difficult background. Adoption is great news, but does come with a special kind of communication to prepare loved ones to be supportive. It will be important for close friends and family members to know that it probably won't be easy, at least not right away. There will be limitations, such as confidentiality rules and the waiting period before adoption is finalized. The possible behavioral challenges might be off-putting to loved ones who aren't prepared to handle it.

As for communication after you have made it through the process and have finally been matched with a child, all communication requires sensitivity to confidentiality expectations. Your child (or children)'s past cannot be an open book shared with all of your social media acquaintances.

Aside from protecting the child's identity, it is also important to protect their story. There are details about their lives that don't need to be broadcast unless your children are mature enough to share it themselves. For example, a child who has been sexually abused might be horrified to find out that everyone in the family and all the friends are aware of her "secret". While explaining her past to others might be good fodder for you to feel like a puffed-up saint, it isn't very good for the child's emotional healing.

Celebrate adoption openly, but maintain your child's past in private as much as possible, unless sharing it is truly necessary (such as in therapy or with a pediatrician).

Note: I have shared my children's past openly in this book. I sought both of their permission prior to writing even a word of their story. They both agreed that potential adoptive families could benefit from truly understanding what adoption feels like to everyone involved.

It's all just a lousy crap-shoot

Occasionally people will ask me questions that they themselves know are awkward. They have to know it's awkward or they wouldn't ask it in a whisper voice like they're sharing state secrets with the Russians. "Aren't you...[*looks around nervously and begins whispering*] ...worried about the child making the same awful choices as their biological parents?" Side note: in awkwardly-whispered questions like this, the words "biological parents" are usually said with a strange emphasis that sounds weirdly-diabolical. Side note to the side note: Most biological parents in the foster scenario aren't diabolical because that would involve being organized enough to work out all the details of a diabolical plan. In my experience, biological parents aren't even organized enough to keep their electricity bill paid.

Yes, I am worried about my children trying out the same choices their biological parents made. Some kids try drugs because they want to see what was so interesting to their parents to be worth losing their kids over. Other kids try drugs to self-medicate for a simmering mental illness.

Worrying about this isn't much different than any parent thinking about their kids' future.

Any parent knows that this whole thing is, at best, a crap-shoot. Sure, you can improve your odds by eating healthy when you're pregnant and following all the doctor's advice. Why else would mothers take football-sized prenatal vitamins and give up both liquor *and* caffeine for 40 weeks?

Your odds of having a healthy, happy child improve even more when you provide a safe, loving home with lots of good training as your babies grow into children and teens. But it's still a total gamble that odds-makers don't want to touch.

You might be able to control how you parent your child, but you can't control genetics (at least you shouldn't because if Hollywood has taught me anything it's that monkeying around with genetically-modified babies is a terrible idea).

Here's an example: I worked for a few years with a terrific woman as my boss. She was educated, classy, and well-respected by her colleagues. Her son had every advantage in sports and parental participation with school events. Her husband coached their son's sports teams and both parents often took off work to take part in school events, like classroom parties.

Unfortunately, all that parental love and attention didn't solve the genetic lottery that her son lost. Hanging high in their family tree was a "bad apple" of mental illness: schizophrenia. No amount of good parenting could solve his growing disease as he became a teen and then adult. He had a revolving door of "interaction" with law enforcement and ended up dropping out of high school. She managed to painfully hold his hand through studying for his GED so he could still try college. That, too, ended in epic failure when he stopped taking his medication, sliding further into the mental illness abyss.

I've interacted with amazing couples who dreamed of a "perfect" child and did everything right, only to end up giving birth to a child with a disability like autism or cerebral palsy, or to lose their child later to a disease like childhood leukemia.

Worry about my children growing up to take drugs (like their parents) definitely affects our decisions in raising them. We talk often about healthy choices and making sure they understand that those choices are 100% within their control. Of course we discuss it when they raise the issue about their own parents' poor choices. We also capitalize on issues that come up in the media or when we see people making poor choices on television.

I grew up in a class full of kids who drank from Thursday night until Sunday morning every week, and several of them experimented with illegal drugs. None of those kids were the product of adoption. Most of them were the children of two-parent households with parents who were respected in the community. They had plenty of advantages in life and yet many of them still chose a path that led, for some, to lifelong addiction and struggle.

None of our efforts as parents of adopted children are a guarantee that they'll heed our advice and follow our training. We can only do what we can do and someday the choice will be up to them. Just like anyone else's children.

Post-adoption record-keeping...(cue dramatic music)

What to do with the post-adoption records was one of the things we didn't prepare for ahead of time and no one warned us about. It isn't terribly dramatic, but helps to know what you're doing.

After adoption is final, you'll have the court decree showing your legal rights as well as the child's name change (if there is one). Even if your child doesn't change their first and middle name, like ours did, you will likely have a change to their last name. That means you will have to change their legal name in the records system at school, at the doctor's office, on their health insurance card, and on their Social Security card.

Our caseworker took care of submitting the documents to change the health insurance card through the state. We submitted copies of the court decree to the school and doctor's office and they made the changes internally.

The biggest challenge was the Social Security card change. In the case of children who have been in foster care, it is possible that biological relatives have used the child's "clean" records to gain credit or apply for anything requiring a credit check. We were advised to check with each credit bureau to make sure our children's identities were not illegally used in the past. Each credit-reporting agency (Experian, TransUnion, and Equifax) required us to submit our request in writing, including the child's date of birth and social security number along with an explanation of why we were seeking to have their credit checked. It took a few weeks to get a reply, but it was worth it to remove our worry about the girls' credit identity.

After hearing from the three credit bureaus, we headed to our local Social Security office to complete the name change process. The process is no different than submitting a name change following marriage or divorce. Bonus Advice #1: I would recommend arriving a few minutes before the doors open so you can be first in line.

I keep all my kids' documents in a pocket folder. Since I have two children, they each get a side of the folder. Documents I keep there include adoption decree, copy of birth certificate, copy of Social Security card, health insurance card, savings account number, known medical history, immunization record, and contact information for their various doctors. If they are on a prescription, I stick a copy in the folder along with the prescription instructions or side effect warnings. I use a business-size envelope to hold the smaller items, like the health insurance cards, so they can't fall out of the folder. I grab the folder whenever we head to the doctor, pharmacy, urgent care, dentist, or any other place I think might request a record. It is handy to have it all in one place.

You will probably be surprised by how many times you will need to show documentation on your children, especially if they are a different race than you. The main thing we often get asked is for proof of guardianship. Some offices look at the child's health insurance card and the driver's license of the parent to see if the last names match. That is often the end of the request. Some offices, however, will ask for proof of guardianship. When fostering, the proof of guardianship will be provided by your caseworker. After adoption, this proof is shown with the birth certificate or adoption decree. Bonus Advice #2: Make peace with this now to avoid frustration later.

What if I adopt a child who is a different race than me?

There are so many different races represented among the ranks of children waiting in foster care. While there is some effort to place children with parents of the same race, it is not always possible. Begin preparing yourself for the possibility that you might end up fostering or adopting a child who is of a different race than you, simply because no other options were available for that child.

Or, as in our case, you might end up with a sibling group that isn't a "matching set", racially speaking. My children share the same mother but have different fathers – and different races.

Your adoption caseworker will likely ask for your preferences as you are going through the adoption licensing process. If you are uncomfortable accepting a particular type of child, you can specify that. For example, you might feel uncomfortable bringing home an African American child if you have family members who are openly racist toward that group. In a case like that, it would be damaging to the child to be treated meanly by his or her new extended family, so such an adoption arrangement would not be in the child's best interest.

If you end up adopting a child who is a different race than you, there will be some effort needed to support their racial heritage. Our family actively works to expose both of our children to African American culture and history as often as possible. We watch movies about it, attend community events, and talk about events in the news that relate to our child's ethnicity. Another family I know has a child adopted from China. They participate in Chinese traditions and holidays, regularly cook Chinese meals, and study Chinese culture.

If you have children of different races, the ones who share your race will often feel the most comfortable. In our situation, there are plenty of opportunities for our Caucasian child to "fit in" with our Caucasian family, but it is more difficult for our bi-racial child to feel the same. Giving her those opportunities requires more effort on our part as parents, but is worth it for our whole family to fully embrace each other.

Are there any books I should read about adoption or parenting?

- ✓ *Adopting the Hurt Child: Hope for families with special-needs kids* by Gregory C. Keck, Ph.D., and Regina M. Kupecky, L.S.W.

- ✓ ***Easy to Love, Difficult to Discipline*** by Becky A. Bailey, Ph.D.
- ✓ ***Parenting with Love and Logic*** by Foster Cline and Jim Fay
- ✓ ***Learning to Slow Down and Pay Attention: A book for kids about A.D.H.D..*** by Kathleen G. Nadeau, Ph.D. and Ellen B. Dixon, Ph.D.
- ✓ ***1-2-3 Magic: 3-Step Discipline for Calm, Effective and Happy Parenting*** by Thomas Phelan
- ✓ ***The A.D.D. Book: New understandings, new approaches to parenting your child*** by William Sears, M.D. and Lynda Thompson, Ph.D.
- ✓ ***The Connected Child*** by Karyn Purvis
- ✓ ***The 5 Love Languages of Children*** by Gary Chapman and Ross Campbell
- ✓ ***Understanding Girls With A.D.H.D..*** by Kathleen G. Nadeau, Ph.D., Ellen B. Littman, Ph.D., and Patricia O. Quinn, M.D.
- ✓ ***When Love is Not Enough: A guide to parenting children with RAD-Reactive Attachment Disorder*** by Nancy L. Thomas

How do I know fostering or adoption is the right fit for my family?

If you have made it this far in the book without giving up, then you are on the right track to deciding of fostering or adoption is right for your family.

This is a major decision and one you shouldn't make lightly. If, after reading this book, you are still interested, then it might be time to meet with a caseworker in your local area to ask some more specific questions and find out the process in your state.

Fostering involves loss for the child, as I mentioned throughout this book, but it also involves loss for you as the foster parent. The goal of fostering is for the child to return home to their biological parents at some point. That means you are stepping into a choice to love a child who you will one day say "good-bye" to forever. I won't lie, this is a very difficult thing to do. Before meeting our girls, my husband and I did a week long emergency respite (think foster-licensed babysitting) for a sibling group of three young kids. We had a lovely week with them and really missed them when they were gone – and that was just one week. I cannot imagine how painful it would have been to foster them for months or even years before "losing" them.

This process is not for the faint-of-heart, but is definitely worth it when you see a child make improvements and begin really discovering what amazing, loving, and fun kids they are.

Some of what you said sounds really difficult. So, is it really worth it?

I have many friends who have given birth and several of them have had terrible pregnancy or birth stories. We're talking 40-weeks of morning sickness or 36-hours of labor kind of bad pregnancy.

But every time, no matter how difficult, these amazing women always say the same thing (usually after recounting how many stitches they had to have after their baby clawed it's way out of her vagina, which doctors claim is a medical term called an "episiotomy"). With a glistening look in their eyes these mothers say, "Oh, it's all worth it when you hold your baby for the first time. I wouldn't change anything about the way it happened."

The same is true for adoption, except for the part with the baby knife-claws and the vagina-stitches.

Nothing about parenting is easy. Just like it isn't easy to deal with morning sickness, breast-feeding a baby who won't latch on, being up all night with a colicky baby, potty training a stubborn child, or dealing with the well-practiced eye-roll of a defiant teen; parenting a child you have adopted is equally challenging in its own special way.

The good news is that I wouldn't change any of it.

The best parts of adoption are the sweet moments when my child rests her head against my shoulder during a movie or gives me a random hug when we're standing in line. I love how Big Sister sometimes says things like "Mom, why don't you go read a book while I clean up these dishes." Or the times when Little Sister spends hours in her room writing lyrics to songs about how loved she feels in our home. It warms my heart when I look over and see them helping each other with homework at the kitchen table or jumping in to help others when we volunteer in the community. It has been so fun to watch them learn new things, play in sports, and celebrate successes – things they might not have done if they hadn't joined our family.

Adoption brings unique struggles, but it also brings amazing blessings as you bond with kids who are goofy, playful, talented, helpful, curious, loving, and unique.

Is it worth it? Definitely. I wouldn't change anything about the way it happened.

Chapter 15
Finishing on a funny note

I'm pretty sure Big just told Little "You should write some more songs tonight....I like hearing them." just so that Little would stay busy in her room and Big could have the TV all to herself.

Little: I just LOVE pandas! Do they have one at the zoo we go to?
Me: No. Pandas are VERY rare. You know, I wonder what God was thinking when He made pandas. They don't seem to have very many natural defenses and they can't even reproduce without the help of a veterinarian.
Husband: How about koalas? Are they that helpless?
Little: That's not what they're called! They're koalalas!
Husband: [*singing to the tune of "Deck the Halls"*] Here's a fat bear, round and jolly – koala-la-la-la-la-la-la-la.

We may not have the most intellectual dinner conversations, but you can't say we aren't entertaining.

Little: [*Playing "Would You Rather" on the drive home tonight*]
Would you rather be a hooker or...
Big: [*interrupting*] Wow! I did NOT expect THAT!
Little: Why? What's a hooker?
Me: Someone who has sex for money.
Little: That's not what I meant. I mean the people who carry all their stuff on their backs!
Me: I'm pretty sure you mean a hobo...

If you were to overhear our conversations with Little you might think we're either practicing our own version of "Who's on First?" or that Little is an elderly Japanese tourist who doesn't fully understand the language and can't hear very well –

>**Me:** Have fun today
>**Little:** Why did you say "See you next Wednesday"?
>**Me:** I said "HAVE. FUN. TO-DAY."

>**Little:** I am NOT VAIN!!! [*dramatic pause*] Now...I'm just going to shoot a video of myself chewing.

About the Author

Confessions of an Instant Mom is the first book by Tina Miller. She earned her masters degree in social work from the University of Missouri-Columbia. Tina is currently a stay-at-home-mom who teaches her children at home, but her career in the "real world" took her primarily into the field of social work and education. She has worked in K-12 settings as well as higher education. An avid reader, Tina's favorite princess is Belle from "Beauty and the Beast" because Belle likes books more than people. Tina's favorite ice cream flavor is Ben and Jerry's "The Tonight Dough". She also has a deeply personal relationship with her pajamas and finds napping to be one of life's great pleasures. The Miller family loves to travel and is currently on a quest to visit all 50 states together.

Made in the USA
Middletown, DE
19 August 2017